Translation and Multilingual Natural Language Processing

Editors: Oliver Čulo (Johannes Gutenberg-Universität Mainz), Silvia Hansen-Schirra (Johannes Gutenberg-Universität Mainz), Stella Neumann (RWTH Aachen), Reinhard Rapp (Johannes Gutenberg-Universität Mainz)

In this series:

1. Fantinuoli, Claudio & Federico Zanettin (eds.). New directions in corpus-based translation studies.

2. Hansen-Schirra, Silvia & Sambor Grucza (eds.). Eyetracking and Applied Linguistics.

3. Silvia Hansen-Schirra, Neumann, Stella & Oliver Čulo (eds.). Annotation, exploitation and evaluation of parallel corpora: TC3 I.

4. Čulo, Oliver & Silvia Hansen-Schirra (eds.). Crossroads between Contrastive Linguistics, Translation Studies and Machine Translation: TC3 II.

5. Rehm, Georg, Felix Sasaki, Daniel Stein & Andreas Witt (eds.). Language technologies for a multilingual Europe: TC3 III.

6. Menzel, Katrin, Ekaterina Lapshinova-Koltunski & Kerstin Anna Kunz (eds.). New perspectives on cohesion and coherence: Implications for translation.

ISSN: 2364-8899

Annotation, exploitation and evaluation of parallel corpora

TC3 I

Edited by

Silvia Hansen-Schirra

Stella Neumann

Oliver Čulo

language
science
press

Silvia Hansen-Schirra, Stella Neumann & Oliver Čulo (eds.). 2017. *Annotation, exploitation and evaluation of parallel corpora: TC3 I* (Translation and Multilingual Natural Language Processing 3). Berlin: Language Science Press.

This title can be downloaded at:
http://langsci-press.org/catalog/book/103
© 2017, the authors

ISBN: 978-3-946234-85-2 (Digital)
   978-3-946234-89-0 (Hardcover)
   978-3-946234-69-2 (Softcover)
ISSN: 2364-8899
DOI:10.5281/zenodo.283376

Cover and concept of design: Ulrike Harbort
Typesetting: Sebastian Nordhoff, Iana Stefanova, Florian Stuhlmann
Proofreading: Aleksandrs Berdicevskis, Alessia Battisti, Alexis Michaud, Alexis Palmer, Anca Gâță, Andreea Calude, Annie Zaenen, Amr El-Zawawy, Ahmet Özdemir, Daniel Riaño, Daniela Kolbe, Eitan Grossman, Elizabeth Zeitoun, Eugeniu Costezki, Ezekiel Bolaji, Francesca Di Garbo, Geert Booij, Hella Olbertz, Ikmi Nur Oktavianti, Julien Heurdier, Kleanthes Grohmann, Lars Zeige, Mario Bisiada, Martin Haspelmath, Matthew Czuba, Natsuko Nakagawa, Pierre-Yves Modicom, Rafael Nonato, Mykel Brinkerhoff, Ulrike Demske, Viola Wiegand, Wafa Abu Hatab
Fonts: Linux Libertine, Arimo, DejaVu Sans Mono
Typesetting software: XƎLᴬTEX

Language Science Press
Habelschwerdter Allee 45
14195 Berlin, Germany
langsci-press.org

Storage and cataloguing done by FU Berlin

Freie Universität Berlin

Contents

Preface to the new edition

This is the first of three volumes which are made up of previously published volumes of the open-access journal "Translation: Computation, Corpora, Cognition" (TC3). Digitalisation has had an immense impact on the way we share our knowledge, including on the way how researchers publish their work. TC3 was one of the very first endeavours to make open-access online publication viable in Translation Studies.

OpenAccess is still being met with quite some scepticism, but we, the former editors of TC3, Silvia Hansen-Schirra, Stella Neumann and Oliver Čulo, believe that the open access to knowledge is the right way to publish scientific results: Research, both for the community and the society at large, often funded by the public and consequently made accessible to the public. The acceptability of research findings is in part determined by how the community as well as the public is informed about this research (both its aims and its achievements).

It can, however, not be taken for granted that the results of up-to-date research are easily and freely accessible to the community or a lay audience. Another problem is to keep pace with the speed of progress in the sciences and an increasing specialization, which widen the gap between the current state of research and the accessibility to published findings. As a counter model to traditional publishing, OpenAccess straightforwardly offers a solution to this problem providing free and online access to cutting-edge, innovative research.

Did we know what we were doing when we started? Well, partially so. Open-Access has had a lot of positive effects on the availability of results and the impact of researchers' work, but in its current, often community-based form, it also poses a challenge for researchers who engage in organising an OpenAccess journal or book series: It is they who are responsible not only for the quality of the contents (which should not and we believe will not diminish in OpenAccess), but for much of the or even the whole appearance, including the design of the publication and the quality of the type setting.

After three years with a special issue every year, the journal TC3 was transformed into the book series now called "Translation and Multilingual Natural Language Processing" (TMNLP) under the roof of LangSci Press. This move reflects in some sense the currently fast-changing publication landscape in both sciences and humanities. Becoming a book series at LangSci has resulted in a boost of the quality of the published volumes. Also, a stringent proofreading process has helped ensure higher consistency within and across the contributions.

The idea to re-publish the TC3 volumes as TMNLP volumes came up very early, with two goals in mind:

- making the works contributed to TC3 available in the long run, beyond just by archiving them somewhere;

- honouring the work which was put into the contributions by re-publishing them under higher quality standards.

The three volumes 3, 4 and 5 are thus not mere re-prints, but the contributions were re-edited according to LangSci guidelines and quality standards. Each volume is introduced by a dedicated introduction from the original volumes. The TC3 contributions are still available in their original format for documentary purposes under http://www.t-c3.org at the time of publication of the corresponding TMNLP volumes. Nevertheless, we believe that re-publication within LangSci will ensure enhanced impact and long-time availability, and on top of that it is a further step into the new world of open-access publishing for Translation Studies.

Germersheim and Aachen, January 2017
Oliver Čulo, Silvia Hansen-Schirra, Stella Neumann

Chapter 1

Introduction

Stella Neumann
IFAAR, RWTH Aachen

Silvia Hansen-Schirra

Oliver Čulo
Johannes Gutenberg-Universität Mainz in Germersheim

1 Parallel corpora in Translation Studies

Parallel corpora, i.e. collections of originals and their translations, can be used in various ways for the benefit of Translation Studies, Machine Translation, Linguistics, Computational Linguistics or simply the human translator. In Computational Linguistics, translation corpora have been employed for Machine Translation but also for term extraction, word sense disambiguation etc. as early as the 1980s (important milestones being Nagao 1984 and Brown et al. 1990). One of the early electronic resources is the Canadian Hansard, which was initially used for implementing sentence alignment (Gale & Church 1991), a task that is now a standard feature of applications such as translation memories. Moreover, parallel corpora are used as data basis for multilingual grammar induction, automatic lexicography and many other tasks in information extraction and language processing across different languages.

In Translation Studies, the focus is more on identifying features that distinguish translations from original texts. From this perspective, the main research interest lies in the detection of patterns of (inevitable) modifications introduced by the translator(s) along the way in terms of local solutions, added information or even larger changes in the register of the text. These modifications may be individual to a given translation task or a translation pair but they may also instantiate typical features of translated text that make translations different from non-translated texts in a wide range of linguistic features. The investigation of

Stella Neumann, Silvia Hansen-Schirra & Oliver Čulo. 2017. Introduction. In Silvia Hansen-Schirra, Stella Neumann & Oliver Čulo (eds.), *Annotation, exploitation and evaluation of parallel corpora*, 1–8. Berlin: Language Science Press. DOI:10.5281/zenodo.283408

corpora is an obvious method to detect these distinctive properties of translations empirically and has been employed since the 1990s as witnessed by Baker (1993; 1996); Johansson & Ebeling (1996) and more recently by Hansen (2003); Teich (2003); Mauranen & Kujamäki (2004) and Hansen-Schirra, Neumann & Steiner (2012). Furthermore, parallel corpora are used as reference works for translation teaching and in professional translation settings since they enable quick and interactive access to translation solutions (e.g. translation memories).

Exchange between the Translation Studies and the Computational Linguistics communities has traditionally not been very intense. Among other things, this is reflected by the different views on parallel corpora. While Computational Linguistics does not always strictly pay attention to the translation direction (e.g. when translation rules are extracted from (sub)corpora which actually only consist of translations), Translation Studies is amongst other things concerned with exactly comparing source and target texts (e.g. to draw conclusions on interference and standardisation effects). However, there has recently been more exchange between the two fields – especially when it comes to the annotation of parallel corpora. This special issue brings together the different research perspectives. Its contributions show – from both perspectives – how the communities have come to interact in recent years.

With issues of the creation of large parallel data collections including multiple annotations and alignments largely solved, the exploitation of these collections remains a bottleneck. In order to use annotated and aligned parallel corpora effectively, the interaction of the different disciplines involved addresses the following issues:

- Query tools: We can expect basic computer literacy from researchers nowadays. However, the gap between writing query or evaluation scripts and program usability is immense. One way to address this is by building web query interfaces. Yet, in general, what are the claims and possibilities for creating interfaces that address a broader public of researchers using multiply annotated and aligned corpora? An additional ongoing question is the most efficient storage form: are database formats superior to other formats?

- Information extraction strategies: The quality of the information extracted by a query heavily depends on the quality of the annotation of the underlying corpus, i.e. on precision and recall of annotation and alignment. Furthermore, the question that arises is how we can ensure high precision and recall of queries (while possibly keeping query construction efficient).

What are the strategies to compose queries which produce high-quality results? How can the query software contribute to this goal?

- Corpus quality: Several criteria for corpus quality have been developed (e.g. in the context of standardisation initiatives). Quality can be influenced before compilation by ensuring the balance of the corpus (in terms of register and sample size), its representativeness etc. Also, inter-annotator agreement and – to a lesser extent – intra-annotator agreement are an issue. But, how can we make the corpora thus created fit for automatic exploitation? This involves issues such as data format validity throughout the corpus, robust (if not 100% correct) processing with corpus tools/APIs and the like. What are relevant criteria and how can they be addressed?

- Corpus maintenance: Beyond the validity of the data format, maintenance of consistent data collections is a more complex task, particularly if the data collection is continually expanded. A change of the annotation scheme entails adjustments in the existing annotation. Questions to this end include whether automatic adjustment is possible and how it can be achieved. Maintenance may also involve compatibility with and/or adaptations to new data formats. How can we ensure sustainability of the data formats?

A colloquium held at the Corpus Linguistics 2009 Conference at the University of Liverpool was concerned with the interface between the requirements of linguists and Translation Studies working with parallel corpora and computational linguists providing the tools and exploiting the corpora for their purposes. In this sense, it was closely related to and a continuation of the workshop "Multilingual Corpora: Linguistic Requirements and Technical Perspectives" held at the Corpus Linguistics 2003 Conference at Lancaster University (see Neumann and Hansen-Schirra Neumann & Hansen-Schirra 2003).

The present special issue is a collection of contributions arising out of this Colloquium. In what follows we outline the contributions responding to some of the questions posed above. The volume sets off with a focus on annotation, alignment and query on the syntactic level: Volk, Marek and Samuelsson discuss a trilingual parallel treebank, the Stockholm Multilingual Treebank SMULTRON. The ultimate purpose of the resource is its exploitation for Machine Translation, a typical application scenario for parallel treebanks. Interestingly, the resource only consists of translations in the three languages English, German and Swedish. The authors discuss solutions for some important questions in querying the treebank, thus focussing on an issue in working with parallel corpora that typically only arises at a later stage of corpus construction but that is not the least trivial.

In their contribution, Vintar and Fišer discuss the exploitation of multilingual resources – and translations in particular – for a monolingual computational linguistic task, the construction and enrichment of the Slovene WordNet. They turn the problem of a lesser-studied language into an advantage in drawing on the rich body of translations existing for Slovene. At various stages of their work, parallel corpora are used to disambiguate word senses with the help of translations – making use of a typical feature of translation, namely settling on one interpretation of ambiguous items in the source text – as well as to extract a bilingual lexicon of word-aligned items in order to enrich the resource with domain-specific lexical items. Vintar and Fišer show how monolingual resources can be successfully exploited with the help of parallel corpora that contain the required information.

Fantinuoli's contribution demonstrates an even more practice-oriented exploitation of corpora, both monolingual and parallel. Fantinuoli describes the design of a software, InterpretBank, which assists conference interpreters in all stages of their work. Based on Baroni and Bernardini's Baroni & Bernardini (2004) Boot-Cat mechanism, it harvests the web for domain-specific documents given a set of search terms, performs term extraction on them and uses additional resources, e.g. Wikipedia or bilingual online dictionaries, to propose definitions, translations, collocations and keyword-in-context information. All available modules, for harvesting, management and retrieval, are adapted to the specific needs of interpreters, reducing the time needed for preparation and allowing for efficient retrieval while interpreting. A pilot module adds the possibility to include parallel resources, e.g. translation memories or the OPUS corpora, in the preparation phase.

The contribution by Čulo, Hansen-Schirra, Maksymski and Neumann revisits a more theory-oriented topic. It discusses the analysis of the bilingual CroCo Corpus, a richly annotated and aligned corpus of English and German translations and originals, with respect to a translation-specific research question. It exemplifies the exploitation of a resource that comes close to a parallel treebank for a research question that has a long history in Translation Studies, namely the study of shifts (e.g. Vinay and Darbelnet Vinay & Darbelnet 1958, Catford Catford 1965 etc.). The goal of this contribution is a heuristic identification of shifts in translation that can then be interpreted as properties of translations. While the main aim of the study is to advance empirical knowledge in the field of Translation Studies, it also has some clear implications for computational handling of translation shifts – for instance, in Machine Translation.

The translation-related research question investigated by Čulo et al. sets the scene for the final paper in this special issue: Alves and Vale introduce an innovative approach to adopting a corpus perspective on psycholinguistic research into the translation process. The authors describe LITTERAE, a computer tool that allows annotating linear representations of the process of producing a translation of a source text. They then proceed to discuss quantitative findings yielded with LITTERAE which suggest certain patterns in target text production. The paper provides a highly interesting way of reducing the gap between corpus-based and process-oriented investigations of translations. It thus rounds off this special issue with a perspective beyond Corpus Linguistics.

The articles in this special issue address a number of the issues discussed above: Vintar and Fišer are concerned with information extraction from various multilingual resources, whereas Čulo et al. exemplify the linguistic interpretation of parallel data on the basis of a heuristic information extraction procedure. Information extraction as well as its interpretation is also exemplified in Alves and Vale's study. Questions of corpus querying are also a major concern of Volk et al, as well as corpus quality, in particular annotation quality. The latter is also addressed by Padó. The only area of interest not covered by one of the contributions is the maintenance of continually expanding resources. This is an area addressed by work in the area of sustainability of corpora, for instance in the framework of the European CLARIN project [1] and similar national initiatives.

2 Acknowledgements

We believe that this volume provides a good overview of some important issues of the operation of parallel corpora, not only focussing on computational issues but also giving insight into the linguistic analysis of translations. If successful, this will not be least thanks to the efforts the reviewers put into providing feedback to the authors and thus ensuring the quality of this issue. The reviewers were: Sabine Bartsch (University of Technology, Darmstadt), Stefan Evert (University of Osnabrück), Johann Haller (IAI, Saarbrücken), Kerstin Kunz (Saarland University, Saarbrücken), Anke Lüdeling (Humboldt University, Berlin), Reinhardt Rapp (University of Mainz, Germersheim), Josef Schmied (University of Technology, Chemnitz), Erich Steiner (Saarland University, Saarbrücken), Elke Teich (Saarland University, Saarbrücken), Mihaela Vela (German Research Center for Artificial Intelligence, Saarbrücken) and Andreas Witt (Institute for the German Language, Mannheim).

We are also grateful to the authors for their contributions and collaboration.

---

[1] http://www.clarin.eu/external/ (last accessed 9 March 2010)

References

Baker, Mona. 1993. Corpus linguistics and translation studies: Implications and applications. In Mona Baker, Gill Francis & Elena Tognini-Bonelli (eds.), *Text and technology: In honour of John Sinclair*, 233–250. Amsterdam & Philadelphia: John Benjamins.

Baker, Mona. 1996. Corpus-based translation studies: The challenges that lie ahead. In Harold Somers (ed.), *Terminology, LSP and translation. Studies in language engineering in honour of Juan C. Sager*, 175–186. Amsterdam: John Benjamins.

Baroni, Marco & Silvia Bernardini. 2004. BootCaT: Bootstrapping corpora and terms from the web. In *Proceedings of LREC2004*, 1313–1316. Lisbon: ELDA.

Brown, Peter F., John Cocke, Stephen A. Della Pietra, Vincent J. Della Pietra, Fredrick Jelinek, John D. Lafferty, Robert L. Mercer & Paul S. Roossin. 1990. A statistical approach to machine translation. *Computational Linguistics* 16(2). 79–85.

Catford, John C. 1965. *A linguistic theory of translation: An essay in applied linguistics.* Oxford: Oxford University Press.

Gale, William A. & Kenneth Ward Church. 1991. Identifying word correspondences in parallel texts. In *Speech and natural language, proceedings of a workshop held at pacific grove, california, usa, february 19-22. 1991*, 152–157. Morgan Kaufmann.

Hansen, Silvia. 2003. *The nature of translated text: An interdisciplinary methodology for the investigation of the specific properties of translations.* Saarbrücken: DFKI/Universität des Saarlandes.

Hansen-Schirra, Silvia, Stella Neumann & Erich Steiner. 2012. *Cross-linguistic corpora for the study of translations: Insights from the language pair English-German.* Berlin: de Gruyter.

Johansson, Stig & Jarle Ebeling. 1996. Exploring the English-Norwegian parallel corpus. In Carol E. Percy, Charles F. Meyer & Ian Lancashire (eds.), 3–16. Amsterdam: Rodopi.

Mauranen, Anna & Pekka Kujamäki (eds.). 2004. *Translation universals.* Amsterdam & Philadelphia: John Benjamins.

Nagao, Makoto. 1984. A framework of a mechanical translation between Japanese and English by analogy principle. In Alick Elithorn & Ranan Banerji (eds.), *Artificial and human intelligence*, 173–180. Amsterdam: North Holland.

Neumann, Stella & Silvia Hansen-Schirra (eds.). 2003. *Proceedings of the Workshop on Multilingual Corpora, Linguistic Requirements and Technical Perspect-*

ives. Corpus Linguistics Conference 2003. Lancaster. http://www.coli.uni-saarland.de/conf/muco03/Proceedings.htm.

Teich, Elke. 2003. *Cross-linguistic variation in system and text: A methodology for the investigation of translations and comparable texts.* Berlin & New York: Mouton de Gruyter.

Vinay, Jean-Paul & Jean Darbelnet. 1958. *Stylistique comparée du français et de l'anglais: Méthode de traduction.* Paris: Didier.

Chapter 2

Building and querying parallel treebanks

Martin Volk

University of Zurich, Institute of Computational Linguistics

Torsten Marek

Yvonne Samuelsson

Stockholm University, Department of Linguistics

This paper describes our work on building a trilingual parallel treebank. We have annotated constituent structure trees from three text genres (a philosophy novel, economy reports and a technical user manual). Our parallel treebank includes word and phrase alignments. The alignment information was manually checked using a graphical tool that allows the annotator to view a pair of trees from parallel sentences. This tool comes with a powerful search facility which supersedes the expressivity of previous popular treebank query engines.

1 Introduction

Recent years have seen a number of initiatives in building parallel treebanks (see Abeillé 2003; Nivre, De Smedt & Volk 2005). The current interest in treebanks is documented in international workshop series like "Linguistically Interpreted Corpora (LINC)" or "Treebanks and Linguistic Theories" (TLT).

We see a treebank as a particular kind of annotated corpus where each sentence is mapped to a special type of graph, a tree which represents its syntactic structure. Traditionally the graphs were constituent structure trees but recent years have also seen dependency treebanks. Constituent structure trees contain nodes and edges where each node holds a label for a group of words (as e.g. NP for noun phrase or VP for verb phrase). Dependency trees represent syntactic dependencies between words directly. We work with constituent structure trees that have labeled edges to denote functional relations which can easily

Martin Volk, Torsten Marek & Yvonne Samuelsson. 2017. Building and querying parallel treebanks. In Silvia Hansen-Schirra, Stella Neumann & Oliver Čulo (eds.), *Annotation, exploitation and evaluation of parallel corpora*, 9–35. Berlin: Language Science Press. DOI:10.5281/zenodo.283438

be mapped to dependencies. The concept of constituent structure trees in tree-banking has been stretched beyond proper trees as defined in graph theory by accepting crossing edges and even secondary edges.

Parallel treebanks are treebanks over parallel corpora, i.e. the "same" text in two or more languages, where one text might be the source text and the other texts are translations thereof, or where all texts are translations of a text outside of the corpus. In addition to the syntactic annotation, a parallel treebank is aligned on the sub-sentential level, for example on the word level or the phrase level.

Parallel treebanks can be created automatically or manually. Automatic creation entails automatic parsing and automatic alignment, both of which will result in a certain amount of error at the current state of the technology. In this paper we focus on the manual creation of parallel treebanks.

Parallel treebanks can be used as training or evaluation corpora for word and phrase alignment, as input for example-based machine translation (EBMT), as training corpora for transfer rules, or for translation studies.

Parallel treebanks have evolved into a research field in the last decade. Cmejrek, Curin & Havelka (2003) at the Charles University in Prague have built a parallel treebank for the specific purpose of machine translation, the Czech-English Penn Treebank with tectogrammatical dependency trees. They have asked translators to translate part of the Penn Treebank into Czech with the clear directive to translate every English sentence with one in Czech and to stay as close as possible to the original.

Other parallel treebank projects include Croco (Hansen-Schirra, Neumann & Vela 2006) which is aimed at building an English-German treebank for translation studies, LinES an English-Swedish parallel treebank (Ahrenberg 2007), and the English-French HomeCentre treebank (Hearne & Way 2006), a hand-crafted parallel treebank consisting of 810 sentence pairs from a Xerox printer manual.

Our group has contributed to these efforts by building a tri-lingual parallel treebank called SMULTRON (Stockholm MULtilingal TReebank). Our parallel treebank consists of syntactically annotated sentences in three languages, taken from translated documents. Syntax trees of corresponding sentence pairs are aligned on a sub-sentential level. On the side we have also experimented with building parallel treebanks for the widely differing languages Quechua and Spanish (Rios, Göhring & Volk 2009).

In this paper we will first describe our parallel treebank and the difficulties in consistent annotation. We have developed a special alignment tool and present its functionality for alignment and search of parallel treebanks. To our knowledge this is the first dedicated tool that combines visualization, alignment and searching of parallel treebanks.

2 Building SMULTRON - The Stockholm MULtilingual TReebank

We have built a trilingual parallel treebank in English, German and Swedish. In its 2008 release SMULTRON consists of around 500 trees from the novel *Sophie's World* and 500 trees from economy texts (an annual report from a bank, a quarterly report from an international engineering company, and the banana certification program of the Rainforest Alliance) (Samuelsson & Volk 2006; 2007). The sentences in Sophie's World are relatively short (14.8 tokens on average in the English version), while the sentences in the economy texts are much longer (24.3 tokens on average; 5 sentences in the English version have more than 100 tokens).

Lately we have added 500 trees from another text genre: a user manual for a DVD player. This genre differs in that it contains a multitude of imperative constructions, many numerical expressions as well as many itemized and enumerated lists. SMULTRON version 2.0 consisting of 1500 trees from three text genres in three languages has been released in the beginning of 2010.[1]

2.1 Monolingual treebanking

For English and German, there are large monolingual treebanks that have resulted in standards for treebanking in these languages. We have followed these standards and (semi-automatically) annotated the German sentences of our treebank with Part-of-Speech tags and phrase structure trees (incl. edges labeled with functional information) according to the NEGRA guidelines (Brants et al. 1997).

For English, we have used the Penn Treebank guidelines which also prescribe phrase structure trees (with PoS tags, but only partially annotated with functional labels). However they differ from the German guidelines in many details. For example, the German trees use crossing edges for discontinuous units while the English trees introduce symbols for empty tokens plus secondary edges for the representation of such phenomena.

There has been an early history of treebanking in Sweden, dating back to the 1970s (cf. Nivre 2002. The old annotation schemes were difficult for automatic

---

[1] SMULTRON is freely available from http://kitt.cl.uzh.ch/kitt/smultron/

processing (in the case of Talbanken, Teleman 1974)[2] or too coarse-grained (in the case of Syntag, Järborg 1986). Therefore we have developed our own treebanking guidelines for Swedish inspired by the German guidelines.

We annotated the treebanks for all three languages separately, with the help of the treebank editor ANNOTATE[3]. ANNOTATE includes the TnT Part-of-Speech Tagger and Chunker for German. We added taggers and chunkers for Swedish and English. After finishing the monolingual treebanks, the trees were exported from the accompanying SQL database and converted into an XML format as input to our alignment tool, the TreeAligner.

Both the German trees and the Swedish trees are annotated with flat structures but subsequently automatically deepened to result in richer and linguistically more plausible tree structures.

2.1.1 Automatic treebank deepening

The German NEGRA annotation guidelines (Brants et al. 1997) result in rather flat phrase structure trees. This means, for instance, no unary nodes, no "unnecessary" NPs (noun phrases) within prepositional phrases and no finite verb phrases. Using a flat tree structure for manual treebank annotation has two big advantages for the human annotator: 1) the annotator needs to make fewer decisions, and 2) the annotator has a better overview of the trees. This comes at the cost of the trees not being complete from a linguistic point of view. One could ask why an NP that consists of only one daughter is not marked, or why an NP that is part of a PP is not marked, while the same NP outside a PP is explicitly annotated. These restrictions also have practical consequences: If certain phrases (e.g. NPs within PPs) are not explicitly marked, then they can only indirectly be searched in corpus linguistics studies.

In addition to the linguistic drawbacks of the flat syntax trees, they are also problematic for phrase alignment in a parallel treebank. Our goal is to align subsentential units (such as phrases and clauses) to get fine-grained correspondences between languages. The alignment focuses on meaning, rather than sentence structure. For example, sentences can have alignment on a higher level of the tree (for instance, if the sentence carries the same meaning in both languages), without necessarily having alignment on all lower levels (for instance, if the sentence contains an NP without direct correspondence in the other language). We

---

[2] Talbanken has recently been cleaned and converted to a dependency treebank by Joakim Nivre and his group. See http://w3.msi.vxu.se/ nivre/research/talbanken.html

[3] Annotate is a treebank editor developed at the University of Saarbrücken. See http://www.coli.uni-sb.de/sfb378/negra-corpus/annotate.html

prefer to have "deep trees" to be able to draw the alignment between the German sentences and the parallel Swedish sentences on as many levels as possible;
in fact, the more detailed the sentence structure is, the more expressive is our
alignment.

We deepened the flat phrase structure trees automatically with a script, which
automatically inserts nodes to create the deeper structure. However, these inser-
tions must be totally unambiguous, so that no errors are introduced. The input
for this program is a tree description in TIGER-XML (König & Lezius 2002), an
interface format which can be created and used by the treebank tool TIGER-
Search[4]. The output is a deepened TIGER-XML tree. We have measured that the
automatic node insertion resulted in an increase of almost 60% additional nodes.

2.1.2 Completeness and consistency checks over treebanks

Completeness and consistency are important characteristics of corpus annotation. Tree completeness means that each token and each node is part of the tree.[5]
This can easily be checked and should ideally be part of the annotation tool.

Consistency checking is more complicated. Consistent annotation means that
the same token sequence (or part-of-speech sequence or phrase sequence) is annotated in the same way across the treebank. Annotation error detection has
been explored for part-of-speech annotation (Dickinson & Detmar Meurers 2003;
Loftsson 2009) and syntactic annotation (Ule & Simov 2004; Dickinson & Meurers 2005).

The variation *n*-gram approach for syntactic annotation (Dickinson & Meurers
2003; 2005) is a method for detecting strings which occur multiple times in the
corpus with varying annotation. The approach can detect bracketing and labeling
errors in constituency annotation.

2.2 Aligning trees

Establishing translation correspondences is a difficult task. This task is traditionally called alignment and is usually performed on the paragraph level, sentence
level and word level. Alignment answers the question: Which part of a text in
language L1 corresponds in meaning to which part of a text in language L2 (under the assumption that the two texts represent the same meaning in different
languages)?

---

[4] See also http://www.ims.uni-stuttgart.de/projekte/TIGER.
[5] Different treebanks take different positions on whether special tokens like punctuation symbols should be part of the tree. For example, the Penn Treebank guidelines require punctuation
marks to be part of the tree, whereas the German TIGER guidelines leave them unattached.

There is considerable interest in automating the alignment process. Automatic sentence alignment of legacy translations helps to fill translation memories. Automatic word alignment is a crucial step in training statistical machine translation systems. Both sentence and word alignment have to deal with 1-to-many alignments, e.g. sometimes a sentence in one language is translated as two or three sentences in the other language.

In other respects sentence alignment and word alignment are fundamentally different. It is relatively safe to assume the same sentence order in both languages when computing sentence alignment. But such a monotonicity assumption is not possible for word alignment which needs to allow for word order differences and thus for crossing alignments. While basic algorithms for sentence alignment can rely on unsophisticated measures like sentence length in characters and still produce good results, word alignment algorithms use cross-language cooccurrence frequencies as a key feature.

Our work focuses on word alignment and on an intermediate alignment level which we call **phrase alignment**. Phrase alignment encompasses the alignment from simple noun phrases and prepositional phrases all the way to complex clauses. For example, on the word alignment level we want to establish the correspondence of the German "verb form plus separated prefix" *fing an* with the English verb form *began*. In phrase alignment, we mark the correspondence of the verb phrases *ihn in den Briefkasten gesteckt* and *dropped it in the mail box*. For the alignment we have developed a specific tool called TreeAligner (Lundborg et al. 2007), which displays two trees and allows the user to draw alignment lines by clicking on phrases and words.

We regard phrase alignment as alignment between linguistically motivated phrases, in contrast to work in statistical machine translation where phrase alignment is defined as the alignment between arbitrary consecutive word sequences. Our phrase alignment is alignment between nodes in constituent structure trees. See Figure 1 for an example of a tree pair with word and phrase alignment. Green lines indicate exact alignments and red lines represent fuzzy alignments (cf.§2.2.2).

It is our belief that linguistically motivated phrase alignment provides useful phrase pairs for example-based machine translation, and provides interesting insights for translation science and cross-language comparisons. Phrase alignments are particularly useful for annotating correspondences of idiomatic or metaphoric language use.

2.2.1 Related research

Our research on word and phrase alignment is related to previous work on word alignment as e.g. in the Blinker project (Melamed 1998) or in the UPLUG project (Lars, Merkel & Petterstedt 2003). Alignment work on parallel treebanks is rare. Most notably there is the Prague Czech-English treebank (Kruijff-Korbayová, Chvátalová & Postolache 2006) and the Linköping Swedish-English treebank (Ahrenberg 2007). There has not been much work on the alignment of linguistically motivated phrases. Tinsley et al. (2007) and Groves, Hearne & Way (2004) report on semi-automatic phrase alignment as part of their research on example-based machine translation.

The most comprehensive study is probably the recent PhD thesis by Zhechev (2009). The author describes his system for automatic phrase alignment over parallel trees which is based on word alignment probabilities provided by GIZA. He evaluates his system against the manually aligned HomeCentre treebank and reports on about 78% recall for 80% precision. These results are comparable to Ambati & Lavie (2008). These approaches are unsupervised in the sense that human-aligned trees are used only for evaluation.

Tiedemann & Kotzé (2009) present a supervised approach which automatically learns phrase alignment features from our parallel treebank. By training on 400 aligned trees and testing on the remaining 100, they report on 80% precision and 76% recall.

Considering the fact that the alignment task is essentially a semantic annotation task, we may also compare our work to other tasks in semantic corpus annotation, for example, the frame-semantic annotation in the German SALSA project (cf. Burchardt et al. 2006).

2.2.2 Our alignment guidelines

We have compiled alignment guidelines for word and phrase alignment between annotated syntax trees. The guidelines consist of general principles, concrete rules and guiding principles. The most important general principles are:

1. Align items that can be re-used as units in a machine translation system.

2. Align as many items (i.e. words and phrases) as possible.

3. Align as close as possible to the tokens.

The first principle is central to our work. The focal point is whether a phrase pair is general enough to be re-used as translation unit in a machine translation

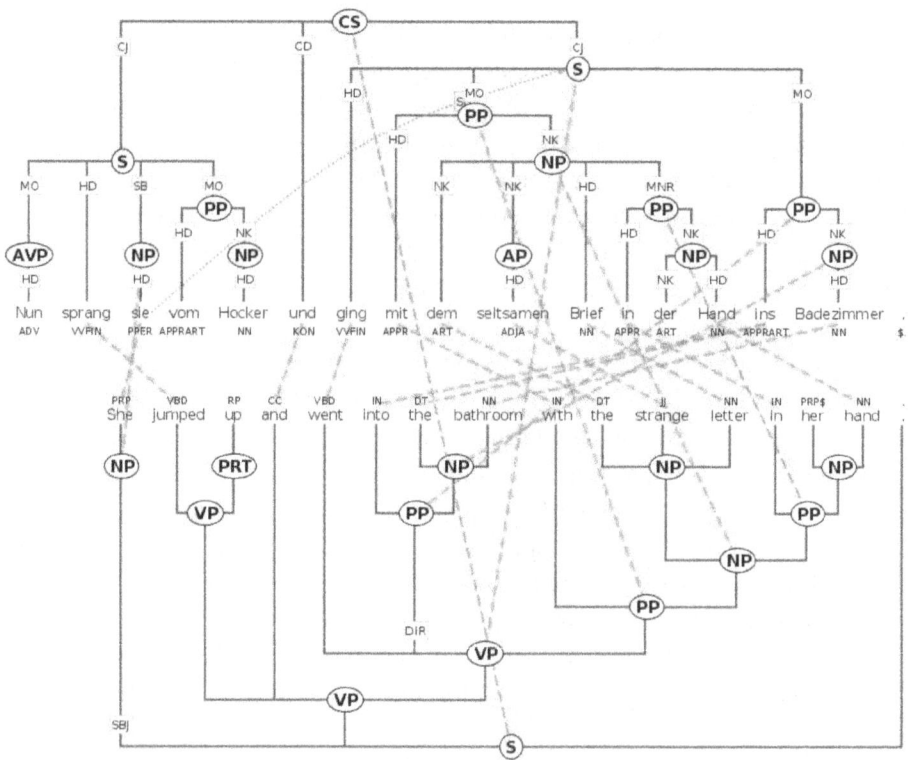

Figure 1: Three pair German-English with word and phrase alignments.

system. For example, in our Sophie's World treebank we have decided not to align *die Verwunderung über das Leben* with *their astonishment at the world* although these two phrases were certainly triggered by the same phrase in the Norwegian original, and both have a similar function in the two corresponding sentences. These two phrases in isolation are too far apart in meaning to license their re-use. We are looking for correspondences like *was für eine seltsame Welt* and *what an extraordinary world* which would make for a good translation in many other contexts.

Some special rules follow from this principle. For example, we have decided that a pronoun in one language shall never be aligned with a full noun in the other, since such a pair is not directly useful in a machine translation system.

Principles 2 and 3 are more technical. Principle 2 tells our annotators that alignment should be comprehensive. We want to re-use as much as possible from the treebank, so we have to look for as many alignments as possible. Principle 3 says that in case of doubt the alignment should go to the node that is closest to the terminals. For example, our German treebank guidelines require a multi-word proper noun to first be grouped in a PN phrase which is a single daughter node of a noun phrase [[Sofie Amundsen]PN]NP. When we align the name, principle 3 tells us to draw the alignment line from the German PN node since it is closer to the tokens than the German NP node.

Often we are confronted with phrases that are not exact translation correspondences but approximate translation correspondences. Consider the phrases *mehr als eine Maschine* and *more than a piece of hardware*. This pair does not represent the closest possible translation, but it represents a possible translation in many contexts. In a way we could classify this pair as the "second-best" translation. To allow for such distinctions we provide our annotators with a choice between exact translation correspondences and approximate correspondences. We also use the term **fuzzy correspondence** to refer to and give an intuitive picture of these approximate correspondences. The option to distinguish between different alignment strengths sounded very attractive at the start. But where and how can we draw the line between exact and fuzzy translation correspondences? We have formulated some clear-cut rules:

- If an acronym is to be aligned with a spelled-out term, it is always an approximate alignment. For example, in our economy reports the English acronym *PT* stands for *Power Technology* and is aligned to the German *Energietechnik* as a fuzzy correspondence.

- Proper names shall be aligned as exact alignments (even if they are spelled differently across languages; e.g. *Sofie* vs. *Sophie*).

But many open questions persist. Is *einer der ersten Tage im Mai* an exact or rather a fuzzy translation correspondence of *early May*? We decided that it is not an exact correspondence. How shall we handle *zu dieser Jahreszeit* vs. *at this time of the year* where a literal translation would be *in this season*? We decided that the former is still an exact correspondence. These examples illustrate the difficulties in distinguishing between exact and approximate translation correspondence. Automatically ensuring the overall consistency of the alignment decisions is a difficult task. We have built a tool to ensure the consistency within the exact and approximate alignment classes. The tool computes the token span for each alignment and checks if the same token span pairs have always received the same alignment type. For example, if the phrase pair *mit einer blitzschnellen Bewegung* and *with a lightning movement* is once annotated as exact alignment, then it should always be annotated as exact alignment. Figure 1 shows approximate alignments between the PPs *in der Hand* and *in her hand*. It was classified as approximate rather than exact alignment since the German PP lacks the possessive determiner.

Currently our alignment guidelines are more than 15 pages long with examples for English-German and English-Swedish alignments. The challenge was to compile precise and comprehensive guidelines to ensure smooth and consistent alignment decisions. In Samuelsson & Volk (2006) we have reported on experiments to evaluate inter-annotator agreement from our alignment tasks. Here we summarize an experiment described in detail in Volk, Marek & Samuelsson (2008) in which we evaluated our alignment guidelines.

2.2.3 Inter-annotator agreement experiments

In order to evaluate the inter-annotator agreement for the alignment task we performed the following experiment. We gave 20 tree pairs in German and English to 12 advanced undergraduate students. Half of the tree pairs were taken from our Sophie's World treebank and the other half from our Economy treebank. We made sure that there was one 1-to-2 sentence alignment in the sample. The students did not have access to the gold standard alignment.

In class we demonstrated the alignment tool to the students, and we introduced the general alignment principles to them. Then the students were given a copy of the alignment guidelines. We asked them to do the alignments independently of each other and to the best of their knowledge according to the guidelines.

Table 1: Alignment Frequencies in the Gold Standard

	Alignment Type	**exact**	**fuzzy**	**total**
Sophie part	word alignment	75	3	78
	phrase alignment	46	12	58
Economy part	word alignment	159	19	178
	phrase alignment	62	9	71

Our own annotation of the 20 tree pairs (the gold standard alignment) contains the alignments shown in Table 1. In the Sophie part of the experiment treebank we have 78 word-to-word alignments and 58 phrase-to-phrase alignments. Note that some phrases consist only of one word and thus the same alignment information is represented twice. We have deliberately kept this redundancy.

The alignments in the Sophie part consist of 125 times 1-to-1 alignments, 4 times 1-to-2 alignments and one 1-to-3 alignment (*wäre* vs. *would have been*) when viewed from the German side. There are 3 times 1-to-2 alignments (e.g. *introducing* vs. *stellte vor*) and no other 1:many alignment when viewed from the English side. In the Economy part the picture is similar.

The student alignments showed a huge variety in terms of numbers of alignments. In the Sophie part they ranged from 125 alignments to bare 47 alignments (exact alignments and fuzzy alignments taken together). In the Economy part, the variation was between 259 and 62 alignments. On closer inspection we found that the student with the lowest numbers works as a translator and chose to use a very strict criterion of translation equivalence rather than translation correspondence. Three other students at the end of the list were not native speakers of either German or English. We therefore decided to exclude these 4 students from the following comparison.

The student alignments allow for the investigation of a number of interesting questions:

- How did the students' alignments differ from the gold standard?

- Which were the alignments done by all students?

- Which were the alignments done by single students only?

- Which alignments varied most between exact and fuzzy alignment?

2.2.4 Inter-annotator agreement results

The remaining 8 students reached between 81% and 48% overlap with our gold standard on the Sophie part, and between 89% and 66% overlap with our gold standard on the Economy texts. This can be regarded as their recall values if we assume that the gold standard represents the correct alignments. These students additionally had between 2 and 22 own alignments in the Sophie part and between 12 and 55 own alignments in the Economy part.

So the interesting question is: What kind of alignments have they missed, and which were the additional own alignments that they suggested (alignments that are not in the gold standard)? We first checked the students with the highest numbers of own alignments. We found that some of these alignments were due to the fact that students had ignored the rule to align as close to the tokens as possible (principle 3 above).

Another reason was that students sometimes aligned a word (or some words) with a node. For example, one student had aligned the word *natürlich* to the phrase *of course* instead of to the word sequence *of course*. Our alignment tool allows that, but the alignment guidelines discourage such alignments. There might be exceptional cases where a word-to-phrase alignment is necessary in order to keep valuable information, but in general we try to stick to word-to-word and phrase-to-phrase alignments.

Another discrepancy occurred when the students aligned a German verb group with a single verb form in English (e.g. *ist zurückzuführen* vs. *reflecting*). We have decided to only align the full verb to the full verb (independent of the inflection). This means that we align only *zurückzuführen* to *reflecting* in this example.

The uncertainties on how to deal with different grammatical forms led to the most discrepancies. Shall we align the definite NP *die Umsätze* with the indefinite NP *revenues* since it is much more common to drop the article in an English plural NP than in German? Shall we align a German genitive NP with an of-PP in English (*der beiden Divisionen* vs. *of the two divisions*)? We have decided to give priority to form over function and thus to align the NP *der beiden Divisionen* with the NP *the two divisions*. But of course this choice is debatable.

When we compute the **intersection** of the alignments done by all students (ignoring the difference between exact and fuzzy alignments), we find that about 50% of the alignments done by the student with the smallest number of alignments is shared by all other students. All of the alignments in the intersection are in our gold standard file. This indicates that there is a core of alignments that are obvious and uncontroversial. Most of them are word alignments.

When we compute the **union** of the alignments done by all students (again ignoring the difference between exact and fuzzy alignments), we find that the number of alignments in the union is 40% to 50% higher than the number of alignments done by the student with the highest number of alignments. It is also about 40% to 50% higher than the number of alignments in the gold standard. This means that there is considerable deviation from the gold standard.

Other discrepancies concern cases of differing grammatical forms, e.g. a German definite singular noun phrase (*die Hand*) that was aligned to an English plural noun phrase (*hands*) in the gold standard but missed by all students. Finally there are a few cases where obvious noun phrase correspondences were simply overlooked by all students (*sich - herself*) although the tokens themselves were aligned. Such cases should be handled by an automated process in the alignment tool that projects from aligned tokens to their mother nodes (in particular in cases of single token phrases).

2.2.5 Working with the TreeAligner

The tree alignments in SMULTRON and in the experiments above were done with a tool called TreeAligner. Let us look at the alignment process in more detail.

When our monolingual treebanks were finished, the trees were exported from the editor system and converted into TIGER-XML, an XML format for encoding syntax graphs with crossing dominance branches and secondary edges. TIGER-XML has been defined as input format for TIGERSearch, a query tool for monolingual treebanks (see §3.1). We use TIGER-XML also as input format for the TreeAligner (Volk et al. 2006).

The TreeAligner program is a graphical user interface to specify (or correct) word and phrase alignments between pairs of syntax trees. [6] The TreeAligner is roughly similar to alignment tools such as I*Link (Ahrenberg, Merkel & Andersson 2002) or Cairo Smith & Jahr it is especially tailored to visualize and align full syntax trees. The TreeAligner is unique in that it allows the alignments of linguistically motivated phrases via node alignments in parallel constituent structure trees (cf. Samuelsson & Volk 2007).

The TreeAligner operates on an alignment file in an XML format developed by us. This file describes the alignments between two TIGER-XML treebanks (specified in the alignment file) holding the trees from language one and language two respectively. For example the alignment between two nodes is represented as:

```
(1)   <align type="good">
         <node treebank_id="de" node_id="s153_11"/>
         <node treebank_id="en" node_id="s144_10"/>
      </align>
```

This says that node 11 in sentence 153 of the German treebank (de) is aligned with node 10 in sentence 144 of the English treebank (en). The node identifiers refer to the IDs in the TIGER-XML treebanks. The alignment is given the label "good" or "fuzzy" depending on the degree of meaning correspondence.

---

[6] The TreeAligner was implemented in Python by Joakim Lundborg and Torsten Marek. It is freely available at http://www.cl.uzh.ch/treealigner.html

The alignment file might initially be empty when we start manual alignment from scratch, or it might contain automatically computed alignments for correction. The TreeAligner displays tree pairs with the trees in mirror orientation (one top-up and one top-down) exemplified in Figure 1. The trees are displayed with node labels, edge labels and part-of-speech tags.

Each alignment is displayed as a dotted line between two nodes (or words) across two trees. Clicking on a node (or a word) in one tree and dragging the mouse pointer to a node (or a word) in the other tree inserts an alignment line. The type of the alignments is represented by its color. Our experiments indicate that eventually more alignment types than just the two used in SMULTRON will be needed to precisely represent fine-grained translation differences. In its most recent version, the TreeAligner supports arbitrarily many alignment types, which can describe many different levels or modes of alignment. These distinctions could prove useful when exploiting the aligned treebanks for Machine Translation and other applications.

Often one tree needs to be aligned to two (or more) trees in the other language. The TreeAligner therefore provides the option to browse the trees independently.

The TreeAligner is designed as a stand-alone tool (i.e. it is not prepared for collaborative annotation). It stores every alignment in an XML file (in the format described above) as soon as the user moves to a new tree pair.

Lately, we have included an interactive module that suggests word and phrase alignments. It follows an alignment memory strategy in analogy to translation memories. This means that the module stores each alignment made by the human annotator. If a new tree pair is to be aligned, the module checks whether any token sequence in the current trees has been previously aligned. If so, it suggests the stored alignment to the annotator.

2.2.6 Consistency checks over alignments

Based on the lessons learned in the inter-annotator agreement experiments, we have improved our alignment guidelines. The question is how we can ensure that the guidelines are followed. We would like to determine whether the alignments are complete and consistent, in similarity to quality checks over treebanks.

For consistency checking of the alignments, we checked for all aligned single tokens and all aligned token sequences whether they are aligned in the same way (i.e. with the predicate 'exact' or 'fuzzy') to the same corresponding tokens. We also checked whether the aligned token sequences differ in length (calculated as number of characters). Large length differences point to possibly erroneous alignments.

Additionally, we examined the cases where different types of nodes are aligned across the languages (e.g., when an adjective phrase in one language is aligned with a prepositional phrase in the other). These consistency checks were initially done manually over an extracted table of the aligned token sequences (with their node labels). This allowed us to sort the token sequences according to different criteria and to abstract away from the dense forest of syntactic information and alignment lines in the TreeAligner.

In order to provide faster feedback about internal alignment link consistency, recent versions of the TreeAligner contain a module for consistency checks that are computed during annotation. We distinguish between two different methods, general structural constraints and association probability. Structural constraints are applied regardless of language or corpus, as they express certain invalid sub-graphs. One structural constraint that has proven useful to the annotators is branch link locality, which demands that if two phrases p_1, p_2 are aligned, any transitive successor of p_1 may only be aligned to a successor of p_2. While there are some systematic problems with this constraint, it is very effective in exposing in-consistencies among the monolingual annotations and spotting simple mistakes.

The other approach relies on measuring association strength between colloc-ates. In our case, we define an alignment link to be our collocate and check if, given the totality of all alignment links in the current corpus, we can reject it as an improbable hypothesis. For this, we use contingency tables and a χ^2 statistic for non-parametric data.

Another (forthcoming) method for consistency checking of alignment draws on the variation n-gram approach for syntactic annotation (Dickinson & Meurers 2003; 2005). It considers alignment as a string-to-string mapping and, treating the target string as a label, examines each source string and their labels, to find inconsistencies in the alignment. Several heuristics are used to filter the set of variations, based on source language context and based on the nature of align-ments in aligned corpora. One additional, complementary, method predicts what phrasal node (if any) a constituent should be aligned to, based on the word align-ment.

3 Searching parallel treebanks

Since the inception of treebanks, many languages and tools for querying syn-tactically annotated corpora have been developed. Most of the tools and query languages have been designed for a specific corpus and a specific annotation format.

Our survey focuses on TGrep and TIGERSearch since they were most influential for our own work. We are well aware of related approaches on searching parallel treebanks such as Nygaard & Johannesen (2004) and Petersen (2006).

3.1 Setting the standard: TGrep and TIGERSearch

TGrep2[7] (Rohde 2005) is a tool for querying structured syntax trees in traditional Penn Treebank "bracketed notation". It supports a wide range of structural operators apart from normal dominance or precedence checks and aims for maximal succinctness of corpus queries. Corpora can be queried using a command line interface, either in interactive or batch mode.

TIGERSearch is a powerful treebank query tool developed at the University of Stuttgart by Wolfgang Lezius (cf. König & Lezius 2002; Lezius 2002a). The TIGER query language is similar in expressiveness to TGrep2, but comes with a graphical user interface and highlighting of the syntax trees, frequency tables for objects identified in the query, and support for exporting query result sets. TIGERSearch has been implemented in Java and is freely available for research purposes. Because of its clearly defined input format and its powerful query language, it has become the corpus query system of choice for many linguists.

The TIGER query language is based on feature-value descriptions of all linguistic objects (tokens and constituents), dominance, precedence and sibling relations in the tree, node predicates (e.g. with respect to token arity and continuity), variables for referencing objects, regular expressions over values for varying the query precision, and queries over secondary edges (which constitute a secondary graph level).

A complex query might look like the following example with > denoting direct dominance, >* denoting general dominance, the dot denoting immediate precedence, and the # symbol introducing variables. This query is meant to find sequences of a noun phrase followed by two prepositional phrases where both PPs are attached to the noun in the NP:

```
(2)   #np:[cat="NP"] >* #n1:[pos="NN"]&
      #np   >   #pp1:[cat="PP"]&
      #n1   .   #pp1&
      #pp1 >* #n2:[pos="NN"]&
      #np   >   #pp2:[cat="PP"]&
      #n2   .   #pp2
```

---

[7] TGrep can be found at http://tedlab.mit.edu/~dr/TGrep2/

This query says: Search for an NP (call it #np) that dominates a noun #n1 (line 1) and two PPs (lines 2 and 5). #pp1 must follow immediately after the noun #n1 (line 3), and #pp2 must follow immediately after the noun within the #pp1 (lines 4 and 6). This query finds, for instance, the German noun phrase "*Die Anhörung vor dem Konkursgericht zur Offenbarungserklärung*" (English "a hearing on the Disclosure Statement before the Bankruptcy Court") where both PPs are attached to the noun "*Anhörung*" in our SMULTRON economy treebank. Like TGrep2, TIGER is a language for querying monolingual treebanks and thus needed to be extended for our goal of querying parallel treebanks. More generally, the design of the input format influences the design of the query language to a large degree, since it defines what can be queried. For instance, the TIGER object model supports crossing branches, leading to non-terminal nodes whose terminal successors are not a proper substring of the sentence. The TIGER query language thus has special functions for dealing with discontinuous nodes. In contrast, the Penn Treebank formalism does not support crossing branches, and thus TGrep2 has no means for this notion.

3.2 The TreeAligner search module

Merz & Volk (2005) listed the requirements for a parallel treebank search tool. Based on these we have re-implemented TIGERSearch for parallel treebanks and integrated it into the TreeAligner.

We allow the power of TIGERSearch queries on both treebanks plus additional alignment constraints. For example, a typical query could ask for a sentence S dominating a prepositional phrase PP in treebank one. This query can be combined with the constraint that the S in treebank one is aligned to a verb phrase VP in treebank two which also dominates a PP. Such a query would be expressed in 3 lines as:

```
(3)  German treebank  #t1:[cat="S"]  > [cat="PP"]
     English treebank #t2:[cat="VP"] > [cat="PP"]
     Alignment        #t1--#t2
```

These three lines are entered into three separate input fields in the user interface (cf. the three input fields in the bottom left in Figure 2). Lines 1 and 2 contain the queries over the two monolingual treebanks. Line 3 contains the alignment constraint. Note that the treebank queries 1 and 2 closely follow the TIGERSearch syntax. In particular they allow the binding of variables (marked with #) to specific linguistic objects in the query. These variables are used in the alignment constraint in line 3. The reuse of the variables is the crucial idea which enabled a clear design of the TreeAligner Search Module by keeping the alignment constraints separate from the queries over the two treebanks.

The above query will find the tree pair in Figure 2 because it matches the alignment between the English VP *closed the front door behind her* and the elliptical German sentence *schloß hinter sich die Tür* (which lacks the subject, but is still annotated as S).

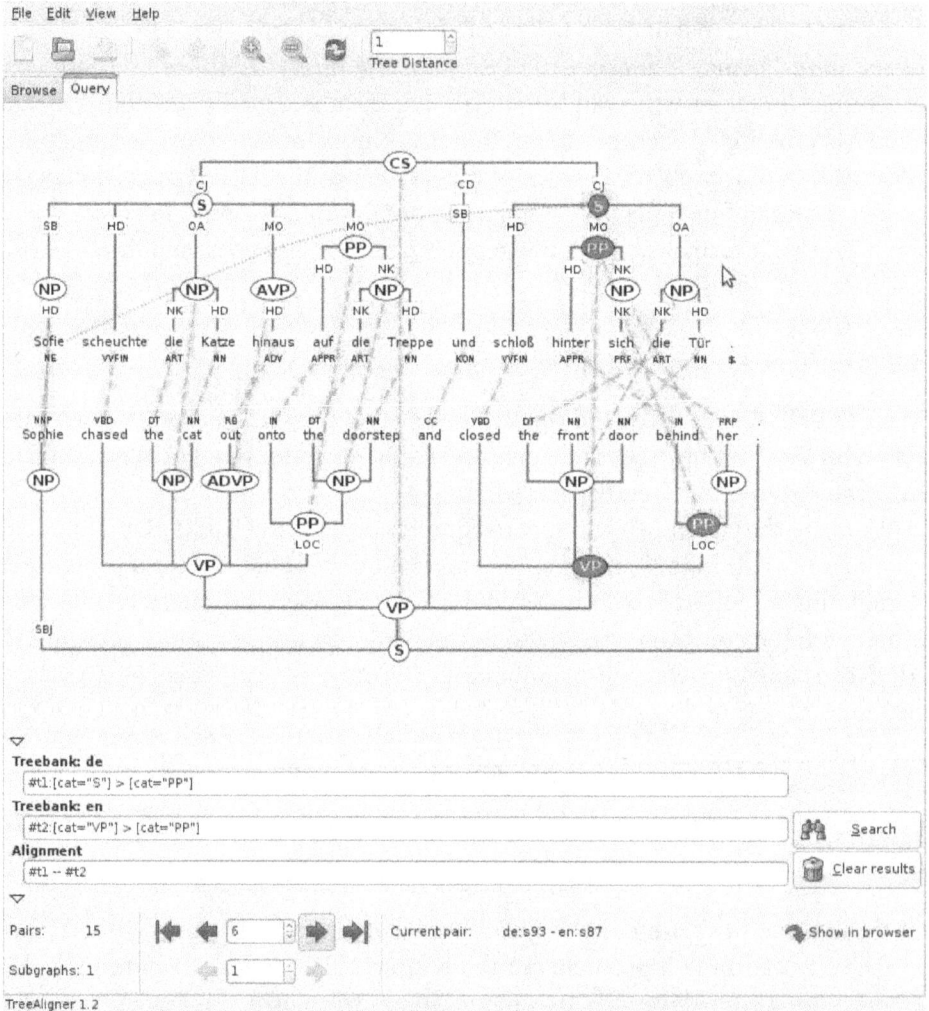

Figure 2: Screenshot of the TreeAligner with the Search Module

The Search Module in the TreeAligner is intended for any parallel treebank where the monolingual treebanks can be converted into TIGER-XML and where the alignment information can be converted to the SMULTRON XML alignment format. The separation of these parts makes it possible to query each treebank separately as well. The system is divided into a monolingual query facility and an alignment query facility that makes use of the former to perform its job. This design choice made it necessary to (re)implement TIGERSearch, the alignment query facility, and the integration into the TreeAligner.

We chose to reimplement TIGERSearch in Python which influenced the feature set. Even though the implementation of TIGERSearch is well documented (in Lezius 2002a among others) and the Java source codes are available under an Open Source license, the reimplementation is not a trivial task.

The query language for the alignment constraints is kept simple as well. The user can specify that two linguistic objects must be aligned (with exact alignment or approximate alignment). And such constraints can be combined with *AND* statements into more complex constraints. We cannot foresee all options on how a parallel treebank will be queried. We have therefore focused on a clear design of the Search Module rather than overloading it with features. This will facilitate the integration of more features as they are requested by users.

3.2.1 Limitations of the TIGER query language

While certain limitations of query languages are due to the original design and could only be approximated, other valid queries may simply be missing from the query language. Lai & Bird (2004) give a list of seven sample queries that each query formalism should support, regardless of the annotation formalism.

Here we deal with queries that contain universal quantification, i.e. selecting a tree by stating constraints over sets of nodes rather than individual nodes. The sample queries contain two examples where this is needed (Lai & Bird 2004):

Q2. Find sentences that do not include the word *saw*.

Q5. Find the first common ancestor of sequences of a noun phrase followed by a verb phrase.

With the TIGER query language and its implementation TIGERSearch (Lezius 2002a), these queries can only be approximated. The result set generated for the approximated queries will likely contain errors.

Because of the technical nature of the discussion in this section we speak of syntax *graphs* rather than trees. These graphs are directed, acyclic and do not contain structure sharing (i.e. each node has exactly one direct ancestor). However, due to crossing branches, TIGER trees cannot be stored as nested lists or XML DOM trees directly, which is the usual understanding of trees.

Node descriptions are boolean expressions of feature constraints of the form "(feature=value)". They are the basis for finding nodes (assignments) in the corpus which are then used for the constraint resolution in TIGER queries.

In the TIGER query language, every node variable is implicitly existentially quantified, i.e. the query

(4) `#s:[cat="S"] !>* #w:[word="saw"]`

returns all combinations of two nodes #s, #w in all graphs, such that #s does not dominate #w (the exclamation mark is the negation operator). From the graphs that were requested in Q2, it will only contain the graphs that do contain the word *saw* outside of an S node. All graphs that do not contain any *saw* will not show up in the result set. Another attempt to formulate Q2 is the query

(5) `#s:[cat="S"] >* #w:[word!="saw"]`

which returns all combinations of all words except *saw* that are dominated by an S node.

Lezius (2002b) already acknowledges this restriction and proposes to extend the TIGER query formalism with a universal quantifier and the implication operator. While this is natural given the unification-based evaluation of queries in TIGERSearch, an implementation comes at great computational cost. For each universal quantifier in a query, all nodes in the graph have to be iterated to find out if they satisfy the implication.

3.2.2 Extensions of the query language in the TreeAligner

The solution suggested by Lezius (2002b) builds upon the query calculus that is at the core of TIGERSearch's query evaluation engine. In contrast, the query engine in the TreeAligner is based on node sets, and combinations of nodes from the different sets to satisfy the constraints given in a query. We summarize our approach in the following. More details can be found in Marek, Lundborg & Volk (2008).

In the previous analysis of Q2, we showed that it is possible to rephrase the query using logical equivalents. Therefore, the query "get all S nodes that do not contain the word *saw* " can be rephrased into "get all graphs where all instances of *saw*, if any, are not dominated by a specific S node". We already demonstrated that it is not possible to express this query within the old formalism, because one of the operands ("all instances of *saw*, if any") is a *set* of nodes rather than a single node. In order to get correct results, we introduce a new type into the query language: the node set.

3.2.3 Node Sets

Traditional node descriptions are still bound by an existential quantifier. A node set, in contrast, is bound by a variable that starts with a percentage symbol:

(6)   `#s:[cat="S"] !>* %w:[word="saw"]`

If one operand in a constraint is a node set instead of a node, the semantics of the constraint are changed. In this case, only those assignments to #s are returned where the constraint holds for each node in the node set %w. In the example at hand, only those S nodes are returned that do not dominate any word *saw* in a graph.

The semantics of the node predicates that are defined in the TIGER query language do not change, they still operate at the node level. In the query

(7)   `%np:[cat="NP"] & tokenarity(%np, 2)`

the node set %np will contain all NPs whose token arity is 2. In other words, the query matches all NPs that consist of two tokens (e.g. "*Cash flow*" or "*this increase*").

If each variable is bound by an existential quantifier, evaluation of a query (or rather, one term in a query in Disjunctive Normal Form) can terminate as soon as one node description does not yield any results. Graphs that do not contain matching nodes for any of the descriptions will also be disregarded. In the presence of node sets, this behavior is wrong. But graphs without any occurrence of *saw* are valid results for the query. Because of that, the semantics of node descriptions bound to node sets are changed. In contrast to nodes, which may not be undefined, they can be the empty set. If this is the case, a constraint is trivially true.

With this change in place, TIGER is in Cantor's paradise, and no one shall expel it from there. With the basic semantics of set types defined, new set predicates can be introduced to refine queries. As an example, consider the query "Return all NPs that do not contain any prepositional phrase PP, but only if the graph contains PPs". With empty node sets allowed, the query would have to be written as

(8) `[cat="NP"] !>* %pp:[cat="PP"] & [cat="PP"]`

to ensure that at least one PP exists. As a side effect, the result set contains one entry for each combination of NP and PP in a matching graph, which is slightly more than what the query was supposed to yield. If a node set must not be empty, set algebra operations like cardinality, element containment, union and intersection could be added to TIGER.

Instead of adding support for set operations, we introduced two new predicates that operate exclusively on node sets: *empty* and *nonempty*. The semantics of the predicates can be inferred from the names, and the previous query can be written in a straightforward manner:

(9) `[cat="NP"] !>* %pp:[cat="PP"] & nonempty(%pp)`

This makes it possible to search for graphs that do not contain a specific kind of nodes by using the predicate *empty*. The query

(10) `%w:[pos="DT"] & empty(%w)`

returns all graphs that do not contain any determiner. For example, in our SMUL-TRON economy treebank we find determinerless English headlines such as "*Group orders grew 8 percent, revenues 10 percent*".

4 Conclusions

We have shown that building parallel treebanks is a complex process. For our SMULTRON treebank we have used separate tools for creating the monolingual treebanks and the alignment. We have improved the process by automatic treebank deepening, interactive visualisation tools, automatic alignment suggestions and consistency checking over trees and alignments.

Still, the process remains burdensome in particular since the alignments constitute semantic annotations. We have shown that good alignment guidelines are important. Our experiments have helped us to realize that the guidelines need to contain a host of fine-grained alignment rules and illustrative examples to clarify critical cases.

Our alignment work would have been impossible without the TreeAligner, our tool for interactive alignment and searching of parallel treebanks. The alignment module provides for quick drag-and-click alignments and supports various views on the aligned trees. The search module allows powerful treebank searches combining constraints over trees and alignments. We have implemented a query language that was inspired by TIGERSearch but which supersedes TIGERSearch with support for universal quantification.

Future research may go in various directions. We would like to move from a split development of monolingual treebanks and subsequent alignment to a more integrated development process. This should include annotation projection and cross-language consistency checks in every phase of the development process. Moreover recent work on automatic word and phrase alignment should be better integrated into the TreeAligner.

Annotating a parallel treebank is labor-intensive, but it provides such a wealth of cross-language observations that make it worthwhile and rewarding.

Acknowledgments

We gratefully acknowledge financial support for the Smultron project by Granholms stiftelse, Rausings stiftelse and the University of Zurich.

References

Abeillé, Anne. 2003. Building and using parsed corpora. In Anne Abeillé (ed.), *Text, speech and language technology*. Dordrecht: Kluwer Academic.

Ahrenberg, Lars. 2007. LinES: An english-swedish parallel Treebank. In *Proceedings of Nodalida 2007*.

Ahrenberg, Lars, Magnus Merkel & Mikael Andersson. 2002. A system for incremental and interactive word linking. In *Proceedings of LREC-2002*, 485–490.

Ambati, Vamshi & Alon Lavie. 2008. Improving syntax driven translation models by re-structuring divergent and non-isomorphic parse tree structures. In *Proceedings of the Student Research Workshop at the Eighth Conference of the Association for Machine Translation in the Americas*.

Brants, Thorsten, Roland Hendriks, Sabine Kramp, Brigitte Krenn, Cordula Preis, Wojciech Skut & Hans Uszkoreit. 1997. *Das NEGRA-Annotationsschema.* Tech. rep. Saarbrücken: Universität des Saarlandes. http://www.coli.uni-sb.de/ sfb378/negra-corpus/negra-corpus.html.

Burchardt, Aljoscha, Katrin Erk, Anette Frank, Andrea Kowalski, Sebastian Padó & Manfred Pinkal. 2006. The SALSA corpus: A German corpus resource for lexical semantics. In *Proceedings of LREC 2006*, 969–974.

Cmejrek, Martin, Jan Curin & Jiří Havelka. 2003. Treebanks in machine translation. In *Proceedings of the 2nd Workshop on Treebanks and Linguistic Theories*, 209–212.

Dickinson, Markus & Walt Detmar Meurers. 2003. Detecting errors in part-of-speech annotation. In *Proceedings of EACL-03*, 107–114.

Dickinson, Markus & Walt D. Meurers. 2003. Detecting inconsistencies in treebanks. In *Proceedings of TLT-03*, 45–56.

Dickinson, Markus & Walt D. Meurers. 2005. Detecting errors in discontinuous structural annotation. In *Proceedings of ACL-05*, 322–329.

Groves, Declan, Mary Hearne & Andy Way. 2004. Robust sub-sentential alignment of phrase-structure trees. In *Proceedings of Coling 2004*, 1072–1078.

Hansen-Schirra, Silvia, Stella Neumann & Michaela Vela. 2006. Multidimensional annotation and alignment in an English-German translation corpus. In *Proceedings of the 5th Workshop on NLP and XML (NLPXML-2006): Multi-Dimensional Markup in Natural Language Processing*, 35–42. Trento: ACL.

Hearne, Mary & Andy Way. 2006. Disambiguation strategies for data-oriented translation. In *Proceedings of the 11th Conference of the European Association for Machine Translation 2006 (EAMT 2006)*, 59–68.

Järborg, Jerker. 1986. *SynTag Dokumentation: Manual för SynTaggning.* Tech. rep. Department of Swedish, Göteborg University.

Kruijff-Korbayová, Ivana, Klára Chvátalová & Oana Postolache. 2006. Annotation guidelines for the Czech-English word alignment. In *Proceedings of LREC 2006*.

König, Ekkehard & Wolfgang Lezius. 2002. *The TIGER language – a description language for syntax graphs. Part 1: User's guidelines.* Tech. rep.

Lai, Catherine & Steven Bird. 2004. Querying and updating treebanks: A critical survey and requirements analysis. In *Proceedings of the Australasian Language Technology Workshop 2004*.

Lars, Ahrenberg, Magnus Merkel & Michael Petterstedt. 2003. Interactive word alignment for language engineering. In *Proceedings of EACL-2003*.

Lezius, Wolfgang. 2002a. *Ein Suchwerkzeug für syntaktisch annotierte Textkorpora.* IMS, University of Stuttgart PhD thesis.

Lezius, Wolfgang. 2002b. TIGERSearch – ein Suchwerkzeug für Baumbanken. In Stephan Busemann (ed.), *Proceedings der 6. Konferenz zur Verarbeitung natürlicher Sprache (KONVENS 2002)*, 107–114.

Loftsson, Hrafn. 2009. Correcting a POS-tagged corpus using three complementary methods. In *Proceedings of EACL-09*, 523–531. Athens.

Lundborg, Joakim, Torsten Marek, Maël Mettler & Martin Volk. 2007. Using the stockholm treealigner. In *Proceedings of the 6th Workshop on Treebanks and Linguistic Theories 2007.*

Marek, Torsten, Joakim Lundborg & Martin Volk. 2008. Extending the TIGER query language with universal quantification. In *Proceedings of KONVENS*, 3–14. Athens.

Melamed, Dan. 1998. *Manual annotation of translational equivalence: The Blinker project.* Tech. rep. 98-06, IRCS. Philadelphia PA.

Merz, Charlotte & Martin Volk. 2005. Requirements for a parallel treebank search tool. In *Proceedings of GLDV-Conference, Sprache, Sprechen und Computer / Computer Studies in Language and Speech 2005.* Peter Lang Verlag.

Nivre, Joakim. 2002. What kinds of trees grow in Swedish soil? A comparison of four annotation schemes for Swedish. In *Proceedings of First Workshop on Treebanks and Linguistic Theory.* Sozopol, Bulgaria.

Nivre, Joakim, Koenraad De Smedt & Martin Volk. 2005. Treebanking in Northern Europe: A white paper. In Henrik Holmboe (ed.), *Nordisk Sprogteknologi. Nordic language technology. Årbog for Nordisk Sprogteknologisk Forskningsprogram 2000-2004*, 97–112. Copenhagen: Museum Tusculanums Forlag.

Nygaard, Lynne & Janne B. Johannesen. 2004. Searchtree: A user-friendly treebank search interface. In *Proceedings of 3rd Workshop on Treebanks and Linguistic Theories*, 183–189.

Petersen, Ulrik. 2006. Querying both parallel and treebank corpora: Evaluation of a corpus query system. In *Proceedings of LREC 2006.*

Rios, Annette, Anne Göhring & Martin Volk. 2009. A Quechua-Spanish parallel treebank. In *Proceedings of the 7th Workshop on Treebanks and Linguistic Theories.*

Rohde, Doug L. T. 2005. *TGrep2 User Manual.* http://tedlab.mit.edu/~dr/Tgrep2/.

Samuelsson, Yvonne & Martin Volk. 2006. Phrase alignment in parallel treebanks. In Jan Hajic & Joakim Nivre (eds.), *Proceedings of the Fifth Workshop on Treebanks and Linguistic Theories*, 91–102.

Samuelsson, Yvonne & Martin Volk. 2007. Alignment tools for parallel treebanks. In *Proceedings of GLDV Frühjahrstagung 2007.*

Smith, Noah A. & Michael E. Jahr. 2000. Cairo: An alignment visualization tool. In *Proceedings of LREC-2000.*

Teleman, Ulf. 1974. *Manual För Grammatisk Beskrivning Av Talad Och Skriven Svenska.* Lund: Studentlitt.

Tiedemann, Jörg & Gideon Kotzé. 2009. Building a large machine-aligned parallel treebank. In *Proceedings of the 8th International Workshop on Treebanks and Linguistic Theories,* 197–208.

Tinsley, John, Ventsislav Zhechev, Mary Hearne & Andy Way. 2007. Robust language pair-independent sub-tree alignment. In *Machine Translation Summit XI Proceedings.*

Ule, Tylman & Kiril Simov. 2004. Unexpected productions may well be errors. In *Proceedings of LREC-04.* Lisbon, Portugal.

Volk, Martin, Torsten Marek & Yvonne Samuelsson. 2008. Human judgements in parallel treebank alignment. In *Proceedings of the COLING Workshop on Human Judgements in Computational Linguistics.* Manchester, UK.

Volk, Martin, Sofia Gustafson-Capková, Joakim Lundborg, Torsten Marek, Yvonne Samuelsson & Frida Tidström. 2006. Xml-based phrase alignment in parallel treebanks. In *Proceedings of EACL Workshop on Multi-dimensional Markup in Natural Language Processing 2006.*

Zhechev, Ventsislav. 2009. *Automatic generation of parallel treebanks: An efficient unsupervised system.* School of Computing at Dublin City University PhD thesis.

Chapter 3

Enriching Slovene wordnet with domain-specific terms

Špela Vintar

Darja Fišer
Dept. of Translation, Faculty of Arts, University of Ljubljana

The paper describes an innovative approach to expanding the domain coverage of the Slovene wordnet (sloWNet) by exploiting multiple resources. In the experiment described here we are using a large monolingual Slovene corpus of texts from the domain of informatics to harvest terminology from, and a parallel English-Slovene corpus and an online dictionary as bilingual resources to facilitate the mapping of terms to sloWNet. We first identify the core terms of the domain in English using the Princeton University's WordNet 2.1, and then we translate them into Slovene using a bilingual lexicon produced from the parallel corpus. In the next step we extract multi-word terms from the Slovene domain-specific corpus using a hybrid approach, and finally match the term candidates to existing wordnet synsets. The proposed method appears to be a successful way to improve the domain coverage of the wordnet as it yields abundant term candidates and exploits various multilingual resources.

1 Introduction

WordNet (Fellbaum 1998) is an extensive lexical database in which words are divided by part of speech and organized into a hierarchy of nodes. Each node represents a concept, and words denoting the same concept are grouped into a synset with a unique id (e.g. ENG20-02853224-n: {car, auto, automobile, machine, motorcar}). Concepts are defined by a short gloss (e.g. 4-wheeled motor vehicle, usually propelled by an internal combustion engine) and are also linked to other relevant synsets in the database (e.g. hypernym: {motor vehicle, automotive vehicle}, hyponym: {cab, hack, taxi, taxicab}). Over time, WordNet has become one of the most valuable resources for a wide range of natural language

Špela Vintar & Darja Fišer. 2017. Enriching Slovene wordnet with domain-specific terms. In Silvia Hansen-Schirra, Stella Neumann & Oliver Čulo (eds.), *Annotation, exploitation and evaluation of parallel corpora*, 35–53. Berlin: Language Science Press. DOI:10.5281/zenodo.283489

processing applications, which initiated the development of wordnets for many other languages as well.[1]

One of such enterprises is the building of sloWNet, the Slovene wordnet (Erjavec & Fišer 2006; Fišer 2007; Fišer & Sagot 2008). While this task would normally involve substantial manual labour and the efforts of several linguists, sloW-Net was built almost single-handedly exploiting multiple multilingual resources, such as bilingual dictionaries, parallel corpora and online semantic resources.

A combination of all these approaches yielded the first version of the Slovene wordnet[2] (sloWNet) containing about 17,000 synsets and 20,000 literals. However, the majority of these literals are single-word items, because the main lexicon extraction procedures involved in the building of a wordnet involved no systematic handling of multi-word expressions. Also, sloWNet can only be as good as the resources that had been used for its construction. While the coverage for some domains, such as botany or zoology, is excellent, other domains remain underrepresented with numerous lexical gaps still to be filled. If we wish to use a wordnet in any domain-specific application, such as Word Sense Disambiguation or Machine Translation, it is crucial that it contains the terminology of the target domain. The purpose of this paper is to propose a method to enrich a wordnet with domain-specific single- and multi-word expressions.

The target domain in the experiments described below is information technology (IT), for which we have a 15 million word monolingual corpus and a small 300,000 word parallel corpus. We use automatic term recognition to extract multi-word IT terms from the large Slovene corpus and word alignment to extract a bilingual lexicon of single-word terms from the parallel corpus. Using this lexicon and a domain-specific bilingual dictionary as a bridge across the two languages we connect the Slovene multi-word terms to the wordnet hierarchy via English, ie. the Princeton WordNet (PWN).

The rest of the paper is organized as follows: first, the sloWNet Project is described. §3 describes the resources used and the procedure to extract domain-specific expressions from the corpus. §4 presents the bilingual part of the experiment where we try to map terms to the wordnet hierarchy. The results are discussed and evaluated in §5, and the paper ends with concluding thoughts and plans for future work.

---

[1] See http://www.globalwordnet.org/gwa/wordnet_table.htm

[2] SloWNet is distributed under the Creative Commons licence, http://nl.ijs.si/slownet

2 Building sloWNet

The first version of the Slovene wordnet was created on the basis of the Serbian wordnet (Krstev et al. 2004), which was translated into Slovene with a Serbian-Slovene dictionary. The main advantages of this approach were the direct mapping of the obtained synsets to wordnets in other languages and the density of the created network. The main disadvantage was the inadequate disambiguation of polysemous words, therefore requiring extensive manual editing of the results. The core sloWNet contains 4,688 synsets, all from Base Concept Sets 1 and 2.

In the process of extending the core sloWNet we tried to leverage the resources we had available, which are mainly corpora. Based on the assumption that translations are a plausible source of semantics we used multilingual parallel corpora such as the Multext-East (Erjavec & Ide 1998) and the JRC-Acquis corpus (Steinberger et al. 2006) to extract semantically relevant information (Fišer 2007).

We assumed that the multilingual alignment based approach can either convey sense distinctions of a polysemous source word or yield synonym sets based on the following criteria (cf. Dyvik 1998, Diab & Resnik 2002 and Ide, Erjavec & Tufis 2002):

(a) senses of ambiguous words in one language are often translated into distinct words in another language (e.g. Slovene equivalent for the English word *school* meaning 'educational institution' is *šola* and *jata* for a large group of fish);

(b) if two or more words are translated into the same word in another language, then they often share some element of meaning (e.g. the English word *boy* meaning a 'young male person' can be translated into Slovene as either *fant* or *deček*).

In the experiment, corpora for up to five languages (English, Slovene, Czech, Bulgarian and Romanian) were word-aligned, with Uplug (Tiedemann 2003) used to generate a multilingual lexicon that contained all translation variants found in the corpus. The lexicon was then compared to the existing wordnets in other languages. For English, the Princeton WordNet (Fellbaum 1998) was used while for Czech, Romanian and Bulgarian, wordnets developed in the BalkaNet project (Tufis 2000) were used. If a match between the lexicon and wordnets across all the languages was found, the Slovene translation was assigned the appropriate synset id. In the end, all the Slovene words sharing the same synset ids were grouped into a synset.

The results obtained in the experiment were evaluated automatically against a manually created gold standard. A sample of the generated synsets was also checked by hand. The results were encouraging, especially for nouns with f-measure ranging between 69 and 81%, depending on the datasets and settings used in the experiment. However, the approach had two serious limitations: first, the automatically generated network contains gaps in the hierarchy where no match was found between the lexicon and the existing wordnets, and second, the alignment was limited to single-word literals, thus leaving out all the multi-word expressions.

We tried to overcome this shortcoming with extensive freely available multi-lingual resources, such as Wikipedia and Eurovoc. These resources are rich in specialized terms, most of which are multi-word. Since specialized terminology is typically monosemous, a bilingual approach sufficed to translate monosemous literals from PWN 2.0 into Slovene. A bilingual lexicon was extracted from Wikipedia, Wiktionary and Wikispecies by following inter-lingual links that relate two articles on the same topic in Slovene and English. We improved and extended this lexicon with a simple analysis of article bodies (capitalisation, synonym extraction, preliminary extraction of definitions). In addition we extracted a bilingual lexicon from Eurovoc, a multilingual thesaurus that is used for classification of EU documents. This procedure yielded 12,840 synsets. The translations of the monosemous literals are very accurate and include many multi-word expressions, and thus neatly complement the previous alignment approach. Also, they mostly contain specific, non-core vocabulary.

Synsets obtained from all three approaches were merged and filtered according to the reliability of the sources of translations. The structure of PWN synsets for which no translation could be found with any of the approaches was adopted from PWN based on the hierarchy preservation principle (Tufis 2000), only the literals were left empty. The entre network of synsets was then formatted in DEBVisDic XML (Horák et al. 2005). The latest version of sloWNet (2.1, 30/09/2009) contains about 20,000 unique literals, which are organized into almost 17,000 synsets, covering about 15% of PWN. Base Concept Sets 1 & 2 are fully covered but there are also many specific synsets. The most frequent domain in sloWNet is Factotum (25%) which was mostly obtained from the dictionary and a parallel corpus, while the following three are Zoology (17%), Botany (13%) and Biology (7%) and come from Wikipedia.

sloWNet mostly contains nominal synsets (91%), and there are some verbal and adjectival synsets as well. Apart from single word literals, there are also quite a few multi-word expressions (43%). These too mostly come from Wikipedia. Synsets in sloWNet are relatively short as 66% of them contain only one literal, average synset length being 1.16 literals. The longest synset contains 16 literals (for verb *goljufati* 'cheat'). The most common relation in sloWNet is hypernymy, which represents almost half of all relations in the wordnet (46%). Hypernymy is by far the most prevalent relation for nouns (91%). Nominal hypernymy chains tend to be quite long, the longest ones containing 16 synsets. Since sloWNet does not cover the entire inventory of PWN concepts, there are some gaps (empty synsets) in the network. An investigation of nominal hierarchies revealed that almost half (46%) of the chains do not contain a single gap and that there are only 2% of chains with five or more gaps. These gaps will have to be filled in the future in order to obtain a denser hierarchy of nodes.

3 Harvesting domain-specific terminology from specialised corpora

3.1 Multi-word expressions and wordnet

Multi-word expressions (MWE) are lexical units that include a range of linguistic phenomena, such as nominal compounds (e.g. *blood vessel*), phrasal verbs (e.g. *put up*), adverbial and prepositional locutions (e.g. *on purpose, in front of*) and other institutionalized phrases (e.g. *de facto*). MWEs constitute a substantial part of the lexicon, since they express ideas and concepts that cannot be compressed into a single word. Moreover, they are frequently used to designate complex or novel concepts. As can be seen in Table 1, the majority of MWEs in the Princeton WordNet do not belong into any of the Basic Concept Sets, meaning that they encode specialized concepts and are frequently terms.

As a consequence, their inclusion into a wordnet is of crucial importance, because any kind of semantic application without appropriate handling of MWEs is severely limited.

Table 1: The distribution of MWEs in PWN across BCS

Group	Frequency
other	64,205
BCS 3	1,470
BCS 2	926
BCS 1	339
total	66,940

For the purpose of MWE identification, various syntactical (Bourigault 1993), statistical (Tomokiyo & Hurst 2003) and hybrid semantic-syntactic-statistical methodologies (Piao et al. 2003, Dias & Nunes 2004) have been proposed, to name but a few. Since the majority of MWEs included in the Princeton WordNet are nominal (see Table 2) and compositional, our approach is based on syntactic features of MWEs.

Table 2: The distribution of MWEs in PWN across part-of-speech (The figures were taken from Princeton WordNet 2.1.)

POS	Frequency
nouns	60,931
verbs	4,315
adverbs	955
adjectives	739
total	66,940

In addressing the issue of MWEs in sloWNet, we initially wanted to find Slovene equivalents for the MWEs already present in Princeton WordNet. We describe this experiment and its successful implementation in (Vintar & Fišer 2008).

3.2 Resources

If a wordnet is to be used in a semantic application within a specific domain, we wish to ensure its coverage within this domain primarily for the target language. The goal we address here is thus how to enrich sloWNet with domain-specific Slovene MWEs regardless of whether their English counterparts are included in PWN or not.

The resources we use to this end are the following (Figure 1):

- Ikorpus, a Slovene corpus of Computer Science texts, size ca. 15 million words, morphosyntactically annotated and lemmatized,

- a Slovene-English parallel corpus of Computer Science abstracts, size ca. 300,000 words, morphosyntactically annotated and lemmatized,

- Islovar, a Slovene-English online dictionary of Computer Science,

- Princeton WordNet.

The idea underlying our approach is that a large domain-specific corpus, especially one sufficiently varied in terms of register and text types, can be an excellent source of domain knowledge. Using terminology extraction, gloss extraction and relation extraction, and mapping these to an existing semantic structure such as a wordnet, can help us construct a valuable domain-specific semantic resource for any language and with minimum manual effort. However, in order to map the extracted terms in the target language onto a wordnet, we need a bilingual resource, preferably a domain-specific one, to provide the links between the source structure (in our case PWN) and the target structure (sloWNet). For our target domain of information science we have compiled a small parallel corpus of scientific abstracts and combined it with a bilingual online dictionary of computer science. Since both of these bilingual resources are used primarily to translate the hypernyms of the extracted terms, the parallel corpus does not need to fulfill all the requirements of a representative corpus.

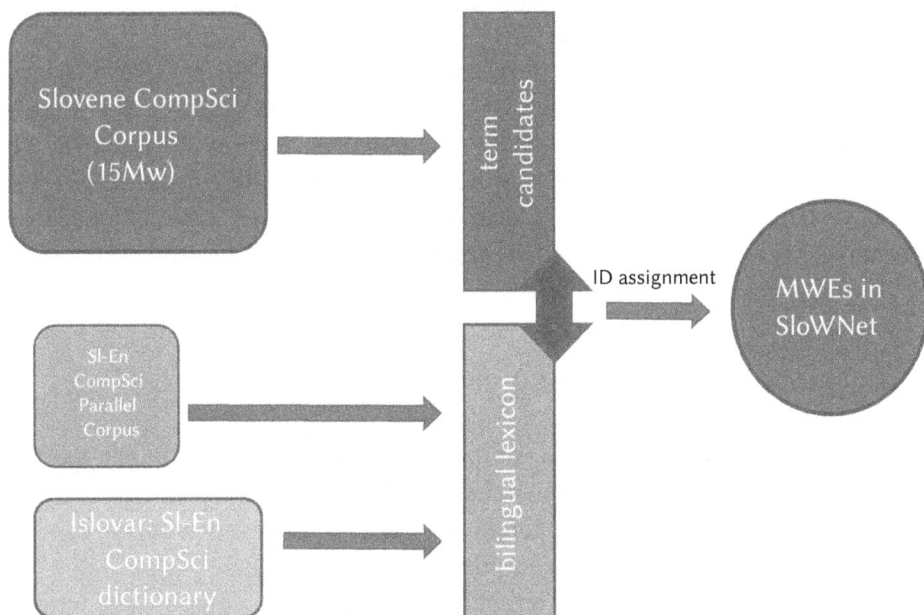

Figure 1: Resources for harvesting MWEs

3.3 Automatic Term Extraction

The domain-specific Ikorpus is composed of texts from five journals dealing with computer science, information and communication technology, and it also con-

tains five consecutive volumes of proceedings of the largest informatics conference in Slovenia (DSI). Its size is approximately 15 million running words, which
makes it an excellent and fairly representative source of terminology.

The task of automatically identifying domain-specific terms in texts has been
addressed by numefrom PWN 2.0 into Slovenerous authors and has been tackled
to the extent that there now exist several commercial tools with term extraction
functionality. The main approaches described in literature range from statistical
ones, where terms are viewed as kinds of collocations, and the challenge lies in
identifying the optimal word dependency measure (Dunning 1993; Daille 1995),
to more linguistically informed and hybrid approaches, where part-of-speech,
morphology and syntax are exploited as indicators of termhood (Heid 1999; Dias
et al. 2000). More recent approaches introduce semantics and utilize context
features to detect terminologically relevant phrases in running text (Maynard &
Ananiadou 1999; Gillam, Tariq & Khurshid 2007), as well as propose methods for
the identification of term variants (Jacquemin 2001). An overview of the trends
is given in Kageura et al. (2004).

In our experiment, automatic term extraction is performed using a hybrid
approach based on morphosyntactic patterns for Slovene and statistical ranking of candidates (Vintar 2004; 2009). The patterns, such as Adjective+Noun
or Noun+Noun[Gen], yield numerous potential MWEs. After candidate phrases
are extracted from the corpora, a term weighting measure is used to assign a
"termhood" value to each phrase. The termhood value W of a candidate term a
consisting of n words is computed as

$$W(a) = \frac{f_a^2}{n} * \sum_{1}^{n} (\log\frac{f_{n,D}}{N_D} - \log\frac{f_{n,R}}{N_R})$$

where f_a is the absolute frequency of the candidate term in the domain-specific
corpus, $f_{n,D}$ and $f_{n,R}$ are the frequencies of each constituent word in the domain-
specific and the general language reference corpus respectively and N_D and N_R
are the sizes of these two corpora in tokens.

The rationale of the termhood measure is that terms are composed of terminologically relevant words, and the measure of terminological relevance is the
comparison of a word's frequency between a domain-specific corpus and a general language corpus. This intuitive notion was first exploited by Ahmad et al.
(1992) and implemented in other term extraction tasks (Scott 1998; Heid et al.
2001), however mostly for single-word terms. We use a modified version of this
idea by adjusting it to multi-word expressions and including the frequency of the
entire expression to override non-terminological phrases occurring only once.

For example, if we compare two phrases a and b, both occurring in the corpus of computer science texts, *spletni brskalnik* 'web browser', (517) and *kakovost izdelka* 'product quality' (74), using the 619-million-words FidaPlus corpus as the source of comparative frequencies we get the following result which indicates that the first phrase is terminologically more relevant than the second:

(1) $W(a) = 517^2/2 * (9.18 + 2.93) = 1618434.89$

(2) $W(b) = 74^2/2 * (1.31 + 1.20) = 6872.38$

The term extraction procedure performed on the 15-million-token Slovene corpus of computer science yielded over 70,000 term candidates of length up to 4 words (Table 3). Given this bulk we can safely assume that not all of them are really terms we would like to include in sloWNet. As it turns out, the candidates list contains a large number of named entities, such as names of software and hardware products, vendors and manufacturers. Since few of these names might be terminologically relevant, we excluded them from further processing. We also employed a frequency threshold and discarded all term candidates which occurred less than 5 times.

The extractor uses morphosyntactic patterns, therefore each multi-word term candidate, e.g. *domenski strežnik* 'domain name server', can be automatically assigned a headword (*strežnik* 'server') and we assume this to be the hypernym of the term candidate.

Table 3: Term candidates and their length in words

MWE size	Number of candidates
2 words (Adj+N, N+N, ...)	54,844
3 words (Adj + Adj + N, N + Prep + N, ...)	16,861
4 words (Adj + Adj + N + N, ...)	2,605
Total	74,310

Clearly, the domain-specific terms constitute a valuable lexical resource, but not until we can introduce some semantic structure. The next step therefore is to integrate at least some of these terms into sloWNet.

4 Mapping terms to sloWNet

At this point we have a large number of Slovene multi-word terms without any semantic information other than the headword of each unit. Thus, for a term such as *prosto programje* 'free software', since it has been extracted through the syntactic pattern Adjective + Noun, we know that *programje* 'software' is the headword and *prosto* the modifier. We may also assume that *programje* is the hypernym of *prosto programje*, and hence we could add *prosto programje* into sloWNet as the hyponym of *programje*, but only if sloWNet already contains the required headword *programje*.

For many multi-word terms this turns out not to be the case, which is why we wish to add both the hypernym and its extracted hyponyms to sloWNet in order to fill as many lexical gaps as possible. We use the Princeton WordNet (PWN) as the source of semantic structure, and to be able to link headwords to this structure we use bilingual lexicon extraction.

4.1 Bilingual lexicon extraction

Bilingual lexicon extraction, also known as word alignment, is a statistical procedure where for each source word a the algorithm computes the probabilities of all of its potential translation equivalents t_1, t_2, t_n in the target language (Och & Ney 2003). The translation equivalents with the highest probability scores are then proposed as entries in the bilingual lexicon. Bilingual lexicon extraction can only be performed on parallel corpora or bitexts.

A small English-Slovene parallel corpus of 300,000 tokens is fed to the Uplug word aligner (Tiedemann 2003), which produces suggested translations for each word found in the corpus. To improve accuracy, we use only alignments of words that occur more than once and alignment scores over 0.05. This yields a bilingual single-word lexicon of 1326 words, mostly nouns (Table 4).

Table 4: Sample entries in the bilingual lexicon

Freq	Score	English	POS	Slovene	POS
4	0.058264988	adaptability	n	prilagodljivost	n
8	0.100445189	additional	a	dodaten	a
5	0.138443460	agent	n	agent	n

In order to improve coverage and accuracy, the automatically extracted bilingual lexicon is further enlarged with entries from the English-Slovene online dictionary of computer science Islovar. The dictionary provides approximately 5,000 bilingual entries and is consulted also in certain cases of ambiguous headword, as described below.

4.2 Adding Terms to sloWNet

For each Slovene multi-word term candidate we first identify its headword and assume that the headword is its hypernym. Using our bilingual lexicon we translate the headword into English and retrieve its synset IDs from PWN. If the headword turns out to be monosemous, the entire group of multi-word terms with the same hypernym can be added to sloWNet under the unique synset ID (Table 5).

Table 5: Monosemous headword

Term candidates	Hypernym, English translation and possible synset IDs	Selected synset ID
prosto programje ('free software') priloženo programje ('attached software') ustrezno programje ('appropriate software') novejše programje ('updated software') dodatno programje ('additional software') vohunsko programje ('spyware')	programje = software ENG20-06162514-n computer_science	ENG20-06162514-n

If the headword could be assigned several possible senses, we exploit the domain label in the wordnet, such as *factotum, biology* etc. If one of the senses of the polysemous headword belongs to the domain Computer Science, then this sense is chosen (Table 6).

If the headword is already part of sloWNet, no disambiguation is needed and the terms can be simply added as hyponyms to the existing Slovene hypernym. Also, in some cases one of the extracted multi-word terms was already in the Islovar dictionary. We can then use the English translation of the term to look up the correct hypernym and synset ID in PWN.

Nevertheless there remain many cases where the polysemous headword does not belong to the CompSci domain in the wordnet and it is neither included in sloWNet or Islovar. In such cases the correct sense must be picked manually (Table 7).

Table 6: Polysemous headword with CompSci domain

Term candidates	Hypernym, English translation and possible synset IDs	Selected synset ID
vgrajena tipkovnica ('built-in keyboard') brezžična tipkovnica ('wireless keyboard') zaslonska tipkovnica ('monitor keyboard') tipkovnica qwerty ('QWERTY keyboard') navidezna tipkovnica ('virtual keyboard') miniaturna tipkovnica ('miniature keyboard') zunanja tipkovnica ('external keyboard') zložljiva tipkovnica ('folding keyboard') ergonomska tipkovnica ('ergonomic keyboard') programska tipkovnica ('program keyboard') slovenska tipkovnica ('Slovene keyboard') modularna tipkovnica ('modular keyboard') alfanumerična tipkovnica ('alphanumeric keyboard')	tipkovnica = keyboard ENG20-03480198-n computer_science ENG20-03480332-n factotum	ENG20-03480332-n

Table 7: Polysemous headword, ID to be selected manually

Term candidates	Hypernym, English translation and possible synset IDs	Selected synset ID
nalaganje gonilnikov ('loading drivers') nalaganje podatkov ('loading data') nalaganje programov ('software download') nalaganje strani ('loading page')	nalaganje = loading ENG20-00671518-n factotum ENG20-13044298-n transport	to be selected manually

5 Discussion

Extracting terms from a large domain-specific Slovene corpus yields the bulk of 74,310 term candidates. We keep only those that occur more than five times and where the headword and its English translation can be identified with reasonable accuracy, and we disregard all names and terms that include names. Some of the remaining terms were already either in the Islovar dictionary or in sloWNet, however the large majority were new. Table 8 shows the number of terms successfully added to sloWNet.

The assumption that the headword of the multi-word expression is at the same time the hypernym of the term may seem daring, however we encountered very

Table 8: Total term candidates added to sloWNet

Category	Number of terms
Already in sloWNet	29
Already in PWN	23
Already in Islovar	198
New	5150
Total	**5400**

few examples where this is not the case. Within a random sample of 200 multi-word terms we found 5 terms where the headword could not be considered an appropriate hypernym of the term, for example a *spletni portal* 'web portal' is not a kind of *portal* 'portal'; *portal* being an architectural term, and *prostor na disku* 'disk space' is not a kind of *prostor* 'space'; although both of these headwords could be used elliptically in a computer science context to mean *web portal* or *disk space* respectively.

As has been described in the previous section, the difficult part is determining the correct sense of the potentially polysemous headword. This ambiguity can of course affect a large number of terms, since – as can be seen in Table 6 – several dozens of multi-word terms share the same headword. While we use all the semantic information we can infer either from the domain label or the online dictionary, nearly half of all the headwords need to be disambiguated manually (Table 9).

Table 9: Categories of headwords

Category	Number of headwords
Monosemous	84
Headwords with CompSci domain	35
Headwords already in sloWNet	11
Headwords derived from MWE PWN	6
To be picked manually	136
Total	**272**

In this respect our methodology could benefit significantly from additional context-based disambiguation procedures. A possible approach would be to use the contexts of the polysemous headwords and compute the semantic similarity between the relevant context words and each sense of the headword. The sense with the greatest semantic similarity to the context features is selected as the correct one. This is essentially a word disambiguation task and various authors have proposed similarity measures based on the graph representation of word-nets (e.g. Leacock & Chodorow 1998; Wu & Palmer 1994; Agirre et al. 2009). In future experiments we plan to implement such methods for the selection of the correct sense.

Finally it should be noted that the domain labels in Princeton WordNet are sometimes illogical, too specific or not specific enough. If we for example explore the financial domain, there is no label [Finance], but we find three different domains for a related set of concepts: *money* [Money], *coin* [Money], *bank* [Banking], *account* [Banking], *pay* [Economy]. This is clearly a problem for automatic text processing, because we cannot rely on the fact that semantically related lexical items share the same domain label in WordNet. On the other hand there exists a hierarchical structure of WordNet domains which was not taken into account in our experiments. It may be the case that some ambiguity issues could be better resolved using this hierarchy.

6 Conclusions

We described an approach to improve the domain coverage of a wordnet by enriching it with semi-automatically extracted multi-word terms. Our method utilizes a combination of mono- and bilingual resources. A large monolingual domain-specific corpus is used as the source of terminology, and a smaller parallel corpus combined with a domain-specific dictionary is used to provide translation equivalents of headwords. These are required in order to map the semantic structure of Princeton WordNet onto the Slovene term candidates and thus integrate them into sloWNet.

Although the approach works well and yields many items of specialised vocabulary, the most difficult part is the selection of the correct sense with polysemous headwords. In some cases the correct sense can be inferred from the domain label or from the dictionary, but in many cases this step still has to be performed manually. In the future we plan to implement a sense disambiguation procedure based on semantic similarity.

It should be noted that an evaluation of monolingual term extraction lies beyond the scope of this paper and is not addressed, although the quality of the term candidates clearly influences the results of the experiment described. Term extraction evaluation depends heavily on the target application, which means that the same system may perform very well in an information retrieval task and poorly in a dictionary-making task. Since the measure of terminological relevance relies on the comparison of relative frequencies between a domain-specific and a reference corpus, the term extraction system performs better for highly specialised domains or, in other words, for terms that do not occur frequently in general language. Information science is in this respect not the ideal domain because IT-related topics are regularly discussed in general language media.

The proposed methodology can be extended to other domains, or indeed other languages. While we employ a specialised monolingual corpus, a bilingual corpus and a specialised bilingual dictionary, the cross-language part of the algorithm is essentially suited to parallel corpora. Especially in domains – or language pairs – for which bilingual dictionaries are scarce it is often more viable to construct a small parallel corpus and use the word-aligned bilingual lexicon to translate headwords. While in other domains we could again exploit the domain labels in WordNet to disambiguate the headword, our methodology is less suitable for general language where polysemy is common and disambiguation can only be performed with context-based methods.

An evaluation of the domain coverage of sloWNet will be performed within a Machine Translation application. In the future we also plan to extend this approach to the extraction of definitions from domain-specific corpora using Machine Learning to distinguish between well-formed and not-well-formed definitions (Fišer, Pollak & Vintar 2010).

References

Agirre, Eneko, Enrique Alfonseca, Keith Hall, AJana Kravalova, Marius Pasca & Aitor Soroa. 2009. A study on similarity and relatedness using distributional and WordNet-based approaches. In *Proceedings of NAACL-HLT 09*. Boulder, USA.

Ahmad, Khurshid, Andrea Davies, Heather Fulford & Margaret Rogers. 1992. What is a term? The semi-automatic extraction of terms from text. In Mary Snell-Hornby, Franz Pöchhacker & Klaus Kaindl (eds.), *Translation studies – an interdiscipline*, 267–278. Amsterdam & Philadelphia: John Benjamins.

Bourigault, Didier. 1993. Analyse syntaxique locale pour le repérage de termes complexes dans un texte. *Traitement Automatique des Langues* 34(2). 105–117.

Daille, Béatrice. 1995. Combined approach for terminology extraction: Lexical statistics and linguistic filtering. In *COLING 94*, 515–521.

Diab, Mona & Philip Resnik. 2002. An unsupervised method for word sense tagging using parallel corpora. In *40th Anniversary Meeting of the Association for Computational Linguistics (ACL-02)*, 255–262. Philadelphia: Association for Computational Linguistics.

Dias, Gaël & Sérgio Nunes. 2004. Evaluation of different similarity measures for the extraction of multiword units in a reinforcement learning environment. In *Proceedings of the 4th International Conference on Languages Resources and Evaluation*, 1717–1721. Lisbon, Portugal.

Dias, Gaël, Sylvie Guilloré, Jean Claude Bassano & José Gabriel Pereira Lopes. 2000. Combining linguistics with statistics for Multiword Term Extraction: A fruitful association? In *Proceedings of 6ème Conférence sur la recherche d'informations assistée par ordinateur (RIAO 2000)*, 1–20. Paris, France.

Dunning, Ted. 1993. Accurate methods for the statistics of surprise and coincidence. *Computational linguistics* 19. 61–74.

Dyvik, Helge. 1998. Translations as semantic mirrors. In *Proceedings of Workshop W13: Multilinguality in the lexicon ii. The 13th biennial European Conference on Artificial Intelligence ECAI 98*, 24–44. Brighton, UK.

Erjavec, Tomaž & Darja Fišer. 2006. Building slovene wordnet. In *Proceedings of the 5th International Conference on Language Resources and evaluation LREC'06*. Genoa, Italy. http://www.lrec-conf.org/lrec2006/nl.ijs.si/et/Bib/LREC06/lrec06-slownet-150.pdf.

Erjavec, Tomaž & Nancy Ide. 1998. The MULTEXT-East corpus. In *Proceedings of the First International Conference on Language Resources and Evaluation, LREC'98*. Granada, Spain.

Fellbaum, Christiane. 1998. *WordNet: An electronic lexical database*. Cambridge: MIT Press.

Fišer, Darja. 2007. Leveraging parallel corpora and existing wordnets for automatic construction of the Slovene wordnet. In *Proceedings of the 3rd Language and Technology Conference L& TC'07*. Poznan, Poland.

Fišer, Darja, Senja Pollak & Špela Vintar. 2010. Learning to mine definitions from Slovene structured and unstructured knowledge-rich resources. In *Proceedings of the 7th Language Resources and Evaluation Conference*. Malta.

Fišer, Darja & Benoît Sagot. 2008. Combining multiple resources to build reliable wordnets. In *Text, Speech and Dialogue Conference (LNCS 2546)*, 61–68. Berlin & Heidelberg: Springer.

Gillam, Lee, Mariam Tariq & Ahmad Khurshid. 2007. Terminology and the construction of ontology. In Fidelia Ibekwe-SanJuan, Anne Condamines & M.

Teresa Cabré Castellví (eds.), *Application-driven terminology engineering*, 49–74. Amsterdam & Philadelphia: John Benjamins.

Heid, Ulrich. 1999. Extracting terminologically relevant collocations from German technical texts. In Peter Sandrini (ed.), *Terminology and knowledge engineering (TKE99)*, 241–255. Vienna: TermNet.

Heid, Ulrich, Stefan Evert, Arne Fitschen, Marion Freese & Andreas Vögele. 2001. *Term candidate extraction in DOT: Dot final report, Part II*. Stuttgart: IMS, University of Stuttgart.

Horák, Aleš, Karel Pala, Adam Rambousek & Martin Povolný. 2005. DEBVisDic – first version of new client-server wordnet browsing and editing tool. In *Proceedings of the Global Wordnet Conference GWA'05*, 325–328. Brno.

Ide, Nancy, Tomaž Erjavec & Dan Tufis. 2002. Sense discrimination with parallel corpora. In *Proceedings of ACL'02 Workshop on Word Sense Disambiguation: Recent successes and future directions*, 54–60. Philadelphia.

Jacquemin, Christian. 2001. *Spotting and discovering terms through Natural Language Processing*. Cambridge, Massachussetts: MIT Press.

Kageura, Kyo, Béatrice Daille, Hiroshi Nakagawa & Lee-Feng Chien. 2004. Introduction: Recent trends in computational terminology. *Terminology* 10(1). 1–21.

Krstev, Cvetana, Gordana Pavlović-Lažetić, Duško Vitas & Ivan Obradović. 2004. Using textual resources in developing Serbian wordnet. *Romanian Journal of Information Science and Technology* 7(1–2). 147–161.

Leacock, Claudia & Martin Chodorow. 1998. Combining local context and WordNet sense similarity for word sense identification. In Christian Fellbaum (ed.), *WordNet: An electronic lexical database*, 265–283. Cambridge: MIT Press.

Maynard, Diana & Sophia Ananiadou. 1999. Term extraction using a similarity-based approach. In Didier Bourigault, Christian Jacquemin & Marie-Claude L'Homme (eds.), *Recent advances in computational terminology*, 261–278. Amsterdam: John Benjamins.

Och, Franz-Josef & Hermann Ney. 2003. A systematic comparison of various statistical alignment models. *Computational Linguistics* 29(1). 19–51.

Piao, Scott, Paul Rayson, Dawn Archer, Wilson Andrew & Tony McEnery. 2003. Extracting multiword expressions with a semantic tagger. In *Workshop on multiword expressions of the 41st ACL meeting*, 49–57. Sapporo, Japan.

Scott, Mike. 1998. Focusing on the text and its key words. In *TALC 98 proceedings*, 152–164. Oxford.

Steinberger, Ralf, Bruno Pouliquen, Anna Widiger, Camelia Ignat, Tomaž Erjavec, Dan Tufiş & Dániel Varga. 2006. The JRC-Acquis: A multilingual aligned parallel corpus with 20+ languages. In *Proceedings of the 5th International Conference on Language Resources and Evaluation*. Genoa, Italy.

Tiedemann, Jörg. 2003. *Recycling translations: Extraction of lexical data from parallel corpora and their application in natural language processing*. Doctoral Thesis. Studia Linguistica Upsaliensia 1 PhD thesis.

Tomokiyo, Takashi & Matthew Hurst. 2003. A language model approach to keyphrase extraction. In *Workshop on Multiword Expressions of the 41st ACL meeting*, 33–41. Sapporo, Japan.

Tufis, Dan. 2000. BalkaNet – design and development of a multilingual Balkan WordNet. *Romanian Journal of Information Science and Technology Special Issue* 7(1–2).

Vintar, Špela. 2004. Comparative evaluation of C-value in the treatment of nested terms. In *Memura 2004 – Methodologies and evaluation of Multiword Units in Real-World Applications (LREC 2004*, 54–57).

Vintar, Špela. 2009. Samodejno luščenje terminologije – izkušnje in perspective. Automatic term recognition – experience and perspectives. In N. Ledinek, M. Žagar Karer & M. Humar (eds.), *Terminologija in sodobna terminografija*, 345–356. Ljubljana: Založba ZRC.

Vintar, Špela & Darja Fišer. 2008. Harvesting multi-word expressions from parallel corpora. In *Proceedings of the 6th International Conference on Language Resources and Evaluation LREC'08*. Marrakech, Morocco.

Wu, Zhibiao & Martha Palmer. 1994. Verb semantics and lexical selection. In *Proceedings of the 32nd Annual Meeting of the Association for Computational Linguistics*. Las Cruces, New Mexico.

Chapter 4

Empty links and crossing lines: Querying multi-layer annotation and alignment in parallel corpora

Oliver Čulo

Silvia Hansen-Schirra

Karin Maksymski
Johannes Gutenberg-Universität Mainz in Germersheim

Stella Neumann
IFAAR, RWTH Aachen

Translation shifts can be informative in various ways. Amongst other things, they can point to typological differences between languages or be indicators of properties of translated text like explicitation or normalisation. Detecting translation shifts in parallel corpora is thus a major task from the viewpoint of translation studies. This paper presents an analysis of translation shifts in a parallel corpus (English-German). It offers an operationalisation of queries which can exploit multi-layer annotation and alignment in order to detect various kinds of translation shifts across category boundary lines and empty alignment links. The paper furthermore discusses the shifts and links them to certain translation properties.

1 Introduction

In both translation studies and contrastive linguistics, multilingual corpora have recently been used to study translation phenomena, i.e. translation shifts or translation properties (as proposed by Baker 1993; 1995; Toury 1995), as well as contrastive differences between languages. One such corpus is the English-German CroCo corpus (Hansen-Schirra, Neumann & Steiner 2012a). The corpus contains

Oliver Čulo, Silvia Hansen-Schirra, Karin Maksymski & Stella Neumann. 2017. Empty links and crossing lines: Querying multi-layer annotation and alignment in parallel corpora. In Silvia Hansen-Schirra, Stella Neumann & Oliver Čulo (eds.), *Annotation, exploitation and evaluation of parallel corpora*, 53–88. Berlin: Language Science Press. DOI:10.5281/zenodo.283498

English and German originals and their translations into German and English, respectively. It can thus be used both as a comparable and a parallel corpus, e.g. to study contrastive differences (e.g. Steiner 2008), translation phenomena (e.g. Čulo et al. 2008; Hansen-Schirra, Neumann & Steiner 2007) or register variation (Neumann 2014). The corpus draws much of its potential from its multi-level stand-off annotation and alignment (Hansen-Schirra, Neumann & Vela 2006).

In this paper, we present a study based on the parallel data in the corpus, exploiting the multi-level alignment in order to detect translation phenomena. We show how the annotation and alignment of linguistic structures can help detect translation phenomena and provide data for their deeper analysis and interpretation. We demonstrate this by presenting data on and interpretations of so-called 'empty links' and 'crossing lines', two phenomena which we characterize in §2.

In §3, we briefly outline the technical background of this study, i.e. the structure of the corpus, the application programmer interface (API) for it and how the corpus was queried. In §4, we discuss the results and possible interpretations of the queries with respect to certain grammatical levels. In §5, we give an overview of possible future directions.

2 Empty links and crossing lines

Approaching translation from a naive perspective, all translation units should match corresponding units in the source texts, both in semantics and in grammatical analysis (Padó 2007). This is, of course, unrealistic, not only because languages diverge, but also because translators make individual decisions. Very broadly speaking, originals and their translations therefore diverge in two respects. Units in the target text may not have matches in the source text and vice versa; thus no connection can be drawn and we speak of *empty links*. Units which do have a counterpart with which they are aligned may be embedded in higher units which are not aligned, resulting in *crossing lines*. This is, for instance, the case when a word is embedded in a chunk with the subject function in one language, and its counterpart in a chunk with the object function.[1] These two concepts are related, on the one hand, to concepts used in formal syntax and semantics, like null elements and discontinuous constituency types in LFG (Bresnan & Kaplan 1982) or HPSG (Pollard & Sag 1994). On the other hand, they

---

[1] The term *crossing line* does not refer to crossing edges in the alignment. The image behind the term is rather that some unit which is embedded in another unit does not follow the alignment path (if there is any) of the higher unit it is embedded in, but "crosses a line" and enters the realm of another unit.

are in the tradition of well-known concepts in translation studies such as one to zero correspondence and translation shifts (Koller 2001; Vinay & Darbelnet 1958; Catford 1965; Newmark 1988; Leuven-Zwart 1989; Cyrus 2006, among others).

We analyze for instance stretches of text contained in one sentence in the source text but spread over two sentences in the target text, as this may have implications for the overall information contained in the target text. We would thus pose a query retrieving all instances where the alignment of the lower level is not parallel to the higher level alignment but points into another higher level unit. In the example below, the German source sequence (1a) as well as the English target sequence (1b) both consist of three sentences which are aligned to each another.

(1)   a. *Aus dem Augenwinkel sah ich, wie eine Schwester dem Bettnachbarn das Nachthemd wechselte. Sie rieb den Rücken mit Franzbranntwein ein und massierte den etwas jüngeren Mann, dessen Adern am ganzen Körper bläulich hervortraten. Ihre Hände ließen ihn leise wimmern.* (GO_FICTION_002)

       b. *Out of the corner of my eye I watched a nurse change his neighbor's nightshirt and rub his back with alcoholic liniment. She massaged the slightly younger man, whose veins stood out blue all over his body. He whimpered softly under her hands.*

In German, the first sentence is subdivided into two clauses, the second one into three. The first English target sentence contains three clauses and the second sentence two. The third sentences in both versions are co-extensive with the clause contained in them. We can see in example (1) that the German clause 3 (*Sie rieb den Rücken mit Franzbranntwein ein*) in sentence 2 is part of the coordinated raising construction (*...and rub his back with alcoholic liniment*) in the English sentence 1. The alignment of this clause points out of the aligned first sentence, thus constituting a crossing line.

The third sentence also contains a crossing line, this time at the levels of grammatical functions and word alignment: the words *Ihre Hände* in the German subject are aligned with the words *her hands* in the English adverbial. However, this sentence is particularly interesting in view of empty links as shown in Hansen-Schirra, Neumann & Vela (2006). The empty links are marked by a black dot in Figure 1.

Our linguistic interpretation is based on a functional view of language. As explained in §3, chunk alignment is based on the mapping of grammatical functions. Hence, the finite *ließen* (word 3) in the German sentence is interpreted as

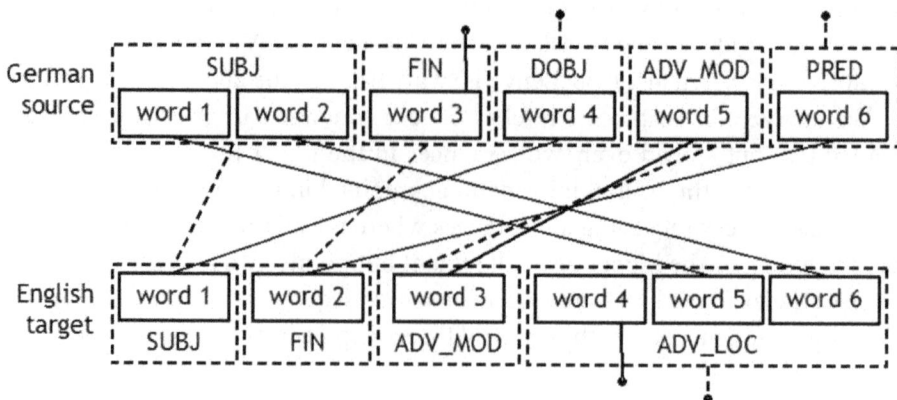

Figure 1: Alignment of grammatical functions and words in sentence 3

a semi-auxiliary and thus as the finite part of the verbal group. Therefore, *wimmern* (word 6) receives the label PRED (for predicator),[2] i.e. the non-finite part of the verb phrase, in the functional analysis. At word level, this German word is linked to word 2 *(whimpered)* in the target sentence, which is assigned FIN, i.e. the finite verb in the layer of grammatical functions. As FIN exists both in the source and in the target sentences, this chunk is aligned. The German functional unit PRED does not have an equivalent in the target text and receives an empty link. Consequently, word 3 in the source sentence *(ließen)* also receives an empty link. This mismatch will be interpreted in view of our translation-oriented research in §4. In the following subsection we will see how these two phenomena can be retrieved automatically.

3 Building and querying the corpus

3.1 Corpus construction

The CroCo corpus consists of English originals (EO), their German translations (GTrans) as well as German originals (GO) and their English translations (ETrans). Both translation directions are represented in 8 registers, with at least 10 texts totaling 31,250 words per register. Altogether, the CroCo Corpus comprises approximately one million words. Additionally, register-neutral reference corpora

---

[2] We are assuming in our annotation an analysis of the verb phrase into *Finite* and *Predicator* following Halliday 1985: 78ff.

are included for German and English, comprising 2,000 word samples from 17 registers.

The corpus thus consists of both a comparable and a parallel part. The registers are political essays (ESSAY), fictional texts (FICTION), instruction manuals (INSTR), popular-scientific texts (POPSCI), corporate communication (SHARE), prepared speeches (SPEECH), tourism leaflets (TOU) and websites (WEB). They were selected because of their relevance for the investigation of translation properties in the language pair English-German. All texts are annotated with

- meta information following the TEI standard (Sperberg-McQueen & Burnard 1994; Burnard & Bauman 2007) including a brief register analysis that allows additional filter options,

- part-of-speech information using the TnT tagger (Brants 2000) with the STTS tag set for German (Schiller et al. 1999) and the Susanne tag set for English (Sampson 1995),

- morphology using MPRO (Maas, Rösener & Theofilidis 2009) which operates on both languages,

- grammatical functions of the highest nodes in the sentence, manually annotated with MMAX2 (Müller & Strube 2006).

Furthermore, all texts are aligned on

- word level using GIZA++ (Och & Ney 2003),

- chunk level (indirectly) by mapping the grammatical functions onto each other,

- clause level (manually) again using MMAX2,

- sentence level using the WinAlign component of the Trados Translator's Workbench (Heyn 1996) with additional manual correction.

The CroCo data are stored in an XML file format based on the corpus encoding standard XCES,[3] a multi-layer stand-off markup format. The CroCoXML format is described in detail in Hansen-Schirra, Neumann & Vela (2006); Hansen-Schirra, Neumann & Steiner (2012b).

---

[3] http://www.xces.org, last visited 3 December 2009

3.2 CroCoAPI

Processing of corpus data – annotation, querying and the like – happens on various linguistic levels and usually involves different applications suited to one particular task (e.g. PoS tagging). Thus, the necessity often arises to convert corpus data into a certain, tool-dependent input format, and then back from the output format to the corpus format. Ideally, a corpus is embedded in some sort of larger framework which manages the data streams or even already comprises a number of applications working in some sort of processing pipeline.

In the case of the CroCo corpus, we created our own *application programming interface* (API) to manage ever more complex queries, including queries operating on multiple annotation and alignment layers, and to apply Java-based annotation tools to the corpus data. The prerequisites for the API were:

- quick integration,

- support of complex queries, also on alignment,

- no complex conversion into other formats required, and

- possibly, integration of multiple formats.

The CroCoAPI presented here is a Java API which includes a light-weight, format-independent data structure that serves as communication interface to other applications. The following paragraphs describe the basic design of the API (Java classes and API layers are typeset in capitals.)

The API is made up of three parts. On top, there is the actual interface CroCoIF, the control methods of which present the basic read/write and iteration calls for the CroCo corpus data. Under the hood, a package called CoReTool is used to represent linguistic structures in stratified layers, and the parallel structures (e.g. aligned words, sentences, etc.) as sets of pairs. As an intermediate level, there is the CroCoXMLIO package, which handles the XCES-based CroCo data format. The CroCoIF communicates with CroCoXMLIO using the CoReTool data structures.

Fundamental within the API is the notion of TEXT. The CORPUS is a collection of TEXTS, and each TEXT contains a thematically coherent set of linguistic structures. The list of available TEXTS can be generated for the whole corpus or per register, as singletons or as pairs of original and translation.

In the multi-layer layout of CroCo, linguistic units like sentences or chunks are defined on the basis of lists of tokens. There is no explicit information about the syntactic hierarchies, e.g. whether a certain chunk belongs to a certain sentence. However, for a number of applications it is helpful or even required to convert this representation into a stratificational structure as provided by CoReTool.

The CoReTool data structure was designed to be a format-neutral representation of the linguistic structures generally found in a corpus. The data structure is used within the CroCoAPI to communicate between the interface and the input-output (IO) level; it can, furthermore, be used as data connector to applications such as the lexical chainer embedded in DKPro (Gurevych et al. 2007, see below). In general, one could enhance the CroCo corpus with various data formats and integrate these with CoReTool; this would only need additional read-/write-methods for handling the different data formats. This stratificational approach is a major difference between the CroCoAPI and other APIs like TigerAPI (Özgür 2007), where programming data structures and underlying data format are more closely linked, and a conversion to TigerXML is necessary for a corpus before using it with any aspects of the TigerAPI.

CoReTool represents the linguistic data in stratified layers, following classical linguistic strata. This differs from the representation in CroCoIF, where all linguistic structures such as sentences or chunks are defined on the basis of tokens.

A Corpus is made up of an ordered collection of Texts, which again is made up of an ordered collection of Sentences, which again is made up of an ordered collection of Tokens. This structure is, so to speak, the backbone of CoReTool and the minimum of data that we expect in a corpus. In addition, a Corpus can be divided into Registers which also relate to collections of Texts (from the Corpus). Likewise, a Sentence can contain Clauses or Chunks which relate to the Tokens of the Sentence. For each of these subunits of a text (including Tokens), it is possible to have aligned counterparts. Every single alignment is represented as a pair; so if unit U is aligned with U' and U'', there will be two pairs $<U,U'>$ and $<U,U''>$.

The CoReTool Java package uses simple data structures like ordered lists to organize the linguistic content it represents. In addition, a couple of basic methods for calculating statistics – e.g. the number of chunk types – are included. The package so far lacks a proper backend-enabled design, so that IO methods could be plugged in on demand. Also, the linguistic representation of CoReTool is currently restricted to syntactic structures.

3.3 Querying the aligned corpus

In CroCoXML, the alignment is stored in one XML file per level. Alignments between words are, for instance, represented as follows:

```
(2)   <word>
          <align xlink:href="#t3076"/>
          <align xlink:href="#t3301"/>
      </word>
      <word>
          <align xlink:href="#t3077"/>
          <align xlink:href="#undefined"/>
      </word>
```

In the pairs of words, the first entry relates to the source text word and the second to the target text word. For the word alignment, we decided to explicitly state empty links by including an element *#undefined* where no corresponding word exists for a source or target language token, which we can read off from the automatic alignment data. This is not the case for the clause or sentence alignment, which was done, or at least corrected, manually.

For the queries on empty links on word level, it would be sufficient to evaluate the XML alignment. A simple way to query for empty links would have been to query the XML annotation for pairs where one element is *#undefined.* However, the implementation results in more abstract ways to query the data. The alignment is read in from the XML files and packed into abstract data structures, representing tokens and token pairs (i.e. aligned tokens), clauses and clause pairs, etc. These abstract data structures are passed on to a query processor. This design allows both for the simple empty link queries and for the more complex crossing line queries. Also, this adheres to our aim of keeping the processing of the corpus format and the processing on linguistic structures separate.[4]

Applied to the parallel sentence from the empty link example in §2, the empty link query returns all German original words which receive an empty link due to a missing equivalent in alignment (in this case *ließen*). The same query can also be applied to the other alignment layers: see §4.1 for empty links at the level of grammatical functions and §4.2 for empty links at clause level.

Querying crossing lines in the aligned source and target sentences combines the alignment on two levels, e.g. word level and the mapping of grammatical functions. Crossing lines are identified, for instance at this level, by querying for words in one grammatical function in one language which are aligned with

---

[4] Partly, the queries are realized on the format-independent CoReTool level. For the most part, however, the queries still use the proprietary CroCoXML API, because the API was still in development at the time of writing and not all levels had been sufficiently and transparently distinguished from one another.

words in a different grammatical function in the other language. An example algorithm (pseudo-code) is given in (3).

```
(3)  for every word_pair in word_pairs
        sl_clause : =
          get_clause(get_sl_word(word_pair))
        tl_clause : =
          get_clause(get_tl_word(word_pair))
        is_aligned?(sl_clause, tl_clause)
     end
```

When applying the query to example (1), it returns the German words *Ihre Hände* which are part of the German subject. They are aligned with the English words *her hands* which are part of the second adverbial. The query for crossing lines between words and grammatical functions is different from other queries, as there is no explicit chunk alignment. When querying for crossing lines between words and clauses, we can make use of the data from the manual clause alignment. Additionally, other alignment layers may be investigated with similar queries, e.g. crossing lines between grammatical functions and clauses.[5]

4 Some selected phenomena

In this section, we will discuss empty links with respect to grammatical functions (§4.1) and clauses (§4.2) as well as crossing lines for words and grammatical functions (§4.3). The three aspects were chosen because they represent a range of queries as well as translation phenomena. The discussion concentrates on the three registers FICTION, SHARE and SPEECH, which show a sufficient range of variation to detect registerial influences on translation properties.

4.1 Empty links at the level of grammatical functions

At the level of grammatical functions, the following tendencies in connection with empty links, i.e. non-aligned segments, can be identified. As Figure 2 shows, percentages for empty links in the translation direction English-German are rather similar for originals and translations, with SHARE exhibiting a slightly

---

[5] It should be noted that precision and recall of the query results can only be as accurate as the word alignment provided by GIZA++ (cf. Čulo et al. 2008). This limits the validity of the query results for crossing lines and empty links on all levels involving word alignment.

higher percentage of unmapped functions for the German translations. When looking at the translations from German to English, however, there is a clear tendency for German texts to exhibit more unmapped functions than the English translations.

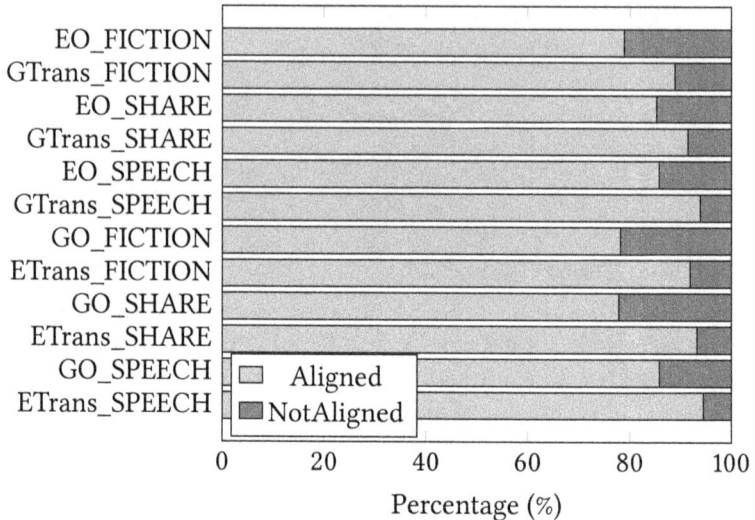

Figure 2: Statistics for alignment of grammatical function

We have chosen the English-German SHARE texts for a closer look at the distribution of empty links for grammatical functions. Table 1 shows the percentage of empty links for the different grammatical functions in EO_SHARE and GTrans_SHARE. Empty links occur with different grammatical functions comparing English and German. The English originals, for example, have more empty links for appositions (APPO) and complements (COMPL), but fewer empty links for predicators (PRED) or modal adverbials (ADVmod). This means that the English original appositions and complements tend to be realized differently in the German translations. Furthermore, the German translated predicators and modal adverbials tend to have other realizations in the source language texts. These differences might be a sign of implicitation or explicitation effects (cf. Hansen-Schirra, Neumann & Steiner 2007). They might, however, also be explained through translation shifts on the level of grammatical functions.

The following examples illustrate the observation that the frequency of empty links for appositions is higher in the English original SHARE texts than in the German translations.

Table 1: Distribution of empty links for grammatical functions (in %)

Tag	Explanation	EO-SHARE	GTrans-SHARE
ADV_CAUSE	causal adverbial (*therefore*)	4.00	0.83
ADV_LOC	locative (*in the house*)	3.72	2.76
ADV_MOD	modal adverbial (*with pleasure*)	4.65	12.02
ADV_TEMP	temporal adverbial (*yesterday*)	3.16	4.97
ADV_OTHER	other adverbials (*however*)	3.53	4.01
APPO	apposition (*..., which makes no sense*)	7.07	0.14
COMPL	complement (*He is a teacher*)	18.51	1.66
CONJ	sentence-initial conjunction (*but*)	7.81	12.85
DOBJ	direct object (*I hit the ball*)	16.19	11.05
FIN	finite part of the verb (*has seen*)	0.19	0.69
IOBJ	indirect object (*Tell him*)	2.51	4.97
NEG	sentence negation (*We didn't go*)	1.12	0.83
MINOR	verbless sentence (*Dear customers!*)	1.3	0.69
PART	particle (*It was just funny*)	2.79	10.91
PRED	non-finite part of verb (*has seen*)	14.6	30.11
PROBJ	prepositional object (*rely on s.o.*)	8.19	0.55
SUBJ	subject (*She is a doctor*)	0.65	0.97

In example (4) the English apposition *a record* is an interpretation of the facts presented in this sentence. Example (5) exhibits a very similar rhetorical move in the apposition *an improvement of 2.3 turns*. In both cases, the appositions are translated by coordinated finite sentences – in the latter one even in inverse order – thus adding linguistic information by spelling out implicit information (cf. Hansen-Schirra, Neumann & Steiner 2007 for more discussion of such phenomena). Obviously, this is one of the sources of empty links between source and target segments.

(4) a. *Revenues rose 11% to $112 billion, a record.* (EO_SHARE_004)

    b. *Der weltweite Umsatz stieg um 11% auf $112 Mrd. und erreichte damit eine neue Rekordhöhe.* (GTrans_SHARE_004)

(5) a. *Working capital turns hit an all-time high of 11.5 - an improvement of 2.3 turns.* (EO_SHARE_004)

    b. *Die Umschlagshäufigkeit des Betriebskapitals konnte um das 2,3 fache gesteigert werden und erreichte die neue Höchstmarke von 11,5.* (GTrans_SHARE_004)

The high frequency of empty links for complements may be due to registerial and typological constraints of the English SHARE texts. Example (6) shows that the English verb *name* is followed by a complement, whereas the German verb *ernannte* is followed by a prepositional object. This is, of course, an obligatory shift due to typological differences between the languages. However, the frequent use of these constructions might be attributed to the register on the basis of a combined interpretation of verb semantics and valency. A possible explanation could then be that companies are supposed to distinguish themselves from other companies and enumerate their achievements. Example (7) again illustrates typological differences between English and German. Whereas English uses a subject complement in the construction *We are pleased...*, the German translation is realized by the finite reflexive verb *(sich) freuen*, but no subject complement, and it is this non-mapping on the level of grammatical functions which creates the empty link here. In terms of "markedness", the original construction is typical of English, just as the translated construction is typical of German, thus explaining the number of empty links for English complements.

(6)   a.   *Also for the second straight year, we were named "The World's Most Respected Company" by the Financial Times.* (EO_SHARE_004)

       b.   *Ebenfalls zum zweiten Mal in Folge ernannte die Financial Times GE zum " am meisten respektierten Unternehmen der Welt".* (GTrans_SHARE_004)

(7)   a.   *We are pleased to present the 2001 Annual Report of the American Institute for Contemporary German Studies (AICGS).* (EO_SHARE_013)

       b.   *Wir freuen uns, Ihnen den Jahresbericht 2001 des American Institute for Contemporary German Studies (AICGS) präsentieren zu können.* (GTrans_SHARE_013)

The high frequency of empty links for predicators in the German translations is due in most cases to typological and register constraints: example (8) illustrates a shift in tense which involves using the predicator, i.e. the non-finite part of the verb phrase *geschafft*. In examples (9) and (10) the English active constructions are translated by passives in German, which include the predicators, the past participles *beschrieben* and *weiterentwickelt*. The choice of passive is motivated by the register since this German specialized register tends to favour a content-oriented style expressed by dense noun phrases as well as passivization (cf. Neumann 2014). Here, typical structures of the target language register are chosen by the translators.

(8) a. *We already have that!* (EO_SHARE_004)

 b. *Das alles haben wir bereits geschafft.* (GTrans_SHARE_004)

(9) a. *In that report, we described several challenges and opportunities that we felt were going to determine the agenda of German-American relations.* (EO_SHARE_013)

 b. *In diesem Bericht werden verschiedene Herausforderungen und Gelegenheiten beschrieben, die unserer Meinung nach die Beziehungen der beiden Staaten bestimmen.* (GTrans_SHARE_013)

(10) a. *It progresses with a drumbeat regularity throughout our business year - year after year.* (EO_SHARE_004)

 b. *Jahr für Jahr wird das Betriebssystem mit der Regelmäßigkeit eines Paukenschlages weiterentwickelt.* (GTrans_SHARE_004)

The reasons for finding more empty links for modal adverbials in the German translations seem to be manifold: example (11) shows an added modal adverbial in the target language text. The back-translation of the German target text reads: *Wireless networks will change the workplace fundamentally.* The English word *transform* is translated through the weaker German verb *verändern* 'change' in combination with the modal adverb *grundlegend* 'fundamentally'. This can be interpreted as a more explicit German version of the English verbal construction.[6] Concerning the modal adverbial *persönlich* (*face-to-face*) in example (12), implicit information in the source text is rendered explicit in the translation. In both cases, however, the translators probably try to emphasize relevant information, thus making the text easier or faster to understand. Example (13) illustrates a case of typologically-driven translation behavior: the English raising construction *continue to benefit* is not available in German (cf. Hawkins 1986: 75ff). Therefore, the translator chose a different lexico-grammatical realization (i.e. the addition of an adverbial), adapting the German translation to target language norms.

(11) a. *Wireless networks will transform the workplace.* (EO_SHARE_005)

 b. *Drahtlose Netzwerke werden den Arbeitsplatz grundlegend verändern.* (GTrans_SHARE_005)

(12) a. *Mostly, it involves creating and distributing paper documents or telephoning and meeting with fellow employees.* (EO_SHARE_005)

---

[6] Cf. Hansen-Schirra, Neumann & Steiner (2007) for a discussion of explicitation vs. addition.

    b. *In den meisten Fällen erstellen und verteilen sie Papierdokumente oder telefonieren oder treffen sich persönlich mit anderen Mitarbeitern.* (GTrans_SHARE_005)

(13)   a. We continue to benefit from the strong natural gas market in North America. (EO_SHARE_002)

    b. Wir profitieren weiterhin von einem starken Erdgasmarkt in Nordamerika. (GTrans_SHARE_002)

In summary, empty links on the level of grammatical functions show some interesting and varied patterns. Some of the empty links may be attributed to different usage patterns, for instance in the case of English complements and German prepositional objects. Others are due to more general contrastive differences such as the (non-)availability of raising constructions in one of the languages, or different kinds of constraints on the mapping from semantic roles to grammatical functions. A more in-depth inspection of all hits for the query could provide an interesting overview of translation properties on this layer.

4.2 Empty links at clause level

For the distribution of empty links at clause level another general tendency can be observed. At clause level, it seems to be a clear characteristic of the English texts to exhibit more empty links. All English original texts as well as all English translations have more empty links than their matching German texts (see Figure 3), with English translations in SPEECH displaying the highest number: here, 35% of the clauses have no link to a clause in the German source text.

When correlating the number of empty links with the total number of clauses, we find a similar picture. In SPEECH as well as in the other registers, the English texts always display a higher number of clauses, although all corpora are of approximately the same size in terms of number of words. Here it is important to bear the following point in mind: the clause segmentation in CroCo is verb-based, i.e. each verb (finite or non-finite) is taken as the basis of a new clause. Thus, empty links occur where a clause (containing a verb) in one text has no direct verbal equivalent in the respective text of the other language either because the content of this clause is expressed in a non-verbal construction or because it is simply left out.

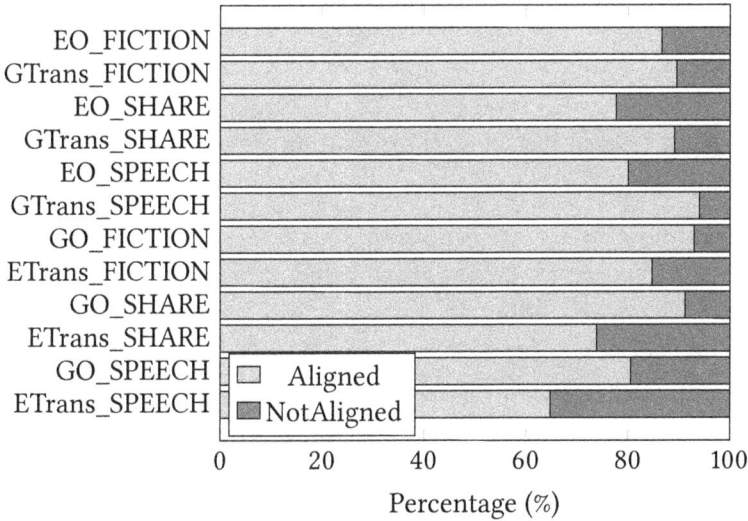

Figure 3: Clause alignment statistics

For the register SPEECH, the numbers are as displayed in Table 2.

The numbers in the second column (aligned clauses) probably represent unproblematic cases, where clauses in the source text can easily be connected to clauses in the target text, perhaps due to similar constructions or rather simple sentences.

The figures in the third column (empty links) leave room for interpretation. Concerning the translation direction German-English, we find that in many cases empty links occur in English subordinate clauses or expressions that resolve more complex structures of the German original text. These are, for example, nominalizations or nouns with premodifying participle constructions, as can be seen in (14) and (15).

Table 2: Clause alignment in SPEECH

	total number clauses	aligned clauses	empty links
GO_SPEECH	3,798	3,058 (80.52%)	740 (19.48%)
ETrans_SPEECH	4,856	3,144 (64.74%)	1,712 (35.26%)
EO_SPEECH	3,853	3,083 (80.02%)	770 (19.98%)
GTrans_SPEECH	3,170	2,981 (94.04%)	189 (5.96%)

(14) a. *[Mittlerweile ist anerkannt,] [dass es zur Sicherung von Beschäftigung vor allem auf Flexibilität ankommt.]* (GO_SPEECH_007)

  b. *[It has now been recognized] [that flexibility is the most important factor] [when it comes] [to safeguarding jobs.]* (ETrans_SPEECH_007)

(15) a. *[Die Staats- und Regierungschefs der Europäischen Union haben in Göteborg erneut ihre Bereitschaft bekräftigt,] [die in Kyoto eingegangenen Verpflichtungen zur Verminderung der Treibhausgase zu erfüllen.]* (GO_SPEECH_001)

  b. *[In Gothenburg the EU heads of state and government reaffirmed their willingness] [to fulfil the commitments] [they made in Kyoto] [to reduce greenhouse gases.]* (ETrans_SPEECH_001)

In both examples, there are only two clauses in the German sentence; these are split into four and three clauses in the respective English translations.[7] In (14), the nominal group *zur Sicherung von Beschäftigung* is transformed into two subordinate clauses with a finite verb (*comes to*) and a non-finite one (*safeguarding*). In (15), the participle of the nominal group *die in Kyoto eingegangenen Verpflichtungen* is translated with the finite verb *made*. This strategy results in one more clause in the English translation than in the German original and therefore in an empty link for this additional clause. There seems to be a tendency within the English translations to use formulations that are more explicit and less dense than those in the German texts. Fabricius-Hansen (1998) reports similar results in a comparison of German source texts and the respective translations into English and Norwegian and discusses a "tendency towards higher informational density that can be observed in German texts of the relevant type and which is correlated with a relatively high degree of syntactic complexity" (Fabricius-Hansen 1998: 197). She relates this phenomenon to different types of discourse information structure, assigning a "hierarchical type" to German texts and an "incremental" one to the English translations (Fabricius-Hansen 1998: 202–203), with the latter increasing incrementality by information splitting (Fabricius-Hansen 1998: 231). In terms of translation properties we could speak of simplification and explicitation here, i.e. a tendency in translations to simplify their texts and to spell things out rather than leaving them implicit (Baker 1996: 180-181). At the same time, the high number of clauses can be interpreted as normalization: the translation (over-)uses typical features of the target language, such as a low informational density (Baker 1996: 183).

---

[7] Clauses are segmented irrespective of their dependence within the syntactic structure. Therefore, embedding cannot be retraced.

Another example where the English translation shows a strong preference for verbal (especially non-finite) instead of nominal constructions is (16), which consists of one single clause in German and of four clauses in English. In the English sentence, the segments form one discontinuous clause with several embedded clauses in between, as marked by the brackets:

(16)   a. *[Mit der am 16. Juli in Bonn beginnenden Klimakonferenz der Vereinten Nationen gehen die jahrelangen Bemühungen um ein verbindliches Klimaschutz-Abkommen in die entscheidende Phase.]*
(GO_SPEECH_001)

       b. *[With the UN Climate Conference [beginning in Bonn on July 16] the many years of efforts [aimed at] [achieving a climate protection agreement] will enter the crucial final phase.]* (ETrans_SPEECH_001)

Here, the German nominal expression *Bemühungen um* is translated with *efforts aimed at achieving*. The decision of the translator to use this construction results in two more clauses in the English sentence: instead of translating the German expression rather literally with *efforts toward*, a longer and more explicit phrasing is used. Again, different types of information structure (hierarchical vs. incremental type, see above) could offer an explanation for the higher number of empty links in the English texts. Additionally, this example illustrates a further reason: the restricted options of English concerning pre- and postmodifying. In the German sentence, the noun *Klimakonferenz* is premodified with the construction *mit der am 16. Juli in Bonn beginnenden*. Since the participle *beginnenden* is used in an adjectival way (as is almost always the case with premodifying participles) it does not form the basis of a new clause. The same information could have been conveyed using a less dense construction, e.g. a postmodifying relative clause like *Mit der Klimakonferenz, die am 16. Juli in Bonn begann*, in this way splitting the sentence into two clauses. For English, all options to translate this sequence result in a postmodifying construction containing a verb.

A considerable number of empty links in the English texts is due to properties of the language system that contrast with German. Here again a connection can be drawn to the translation property of normalization: Teich (2003: 218) relates this to contrastive differences in the range of options available in source and target language, positing that fewer options in the target language entail compensations which may then lead to normalization. English has fewer options compared to German with respect to pre- and postmodification, which leads to normalization. That in turn would explain at least in part the high number of empty links.

Still another explanation could be different registerial restrictions. In example (17), the German adverb *deshalb* is translated with the expression *that is why*, again resulting in an additional clause in the English text:

(17)   a.   *[Deshalb machen hohe Abgaben Arbeit teuer] [und können doch nicht verhindern,] [dass unseren Sozialsystemen der Kollaps droht.]* (GO_SPEECH_007)

   b.   *[That is why] [high taxes make work expensive] [and yet cannot protect our social system from] [impending collapse.]* (ETrans_SPEECH_007)

It is possible that the use of *therefore* instead of *that is why* would sound too formal for a speech or that a more explicit reference to the previous sentence has to be made. In any case, this is an example for a situation in which the individual decision of the translator influences the number of empty links. If this proves to be a typical pattern (all three occurrences of *that is why* are in fact translations of *deshalb*), it can be interpreted as a possible sign of explicitation because it shows a "rise in the level of cohesive explicitness" (Blum-Kulka 1986: 19).

For the translation direction English-German in SPEECH the picture is a different one, with only 5.96% of empty links in the target texts (GTrans_SPEECH). These are mainly cases where the translator has to opt for a different translation because of lexical differences of the verb as in (16) or where s/he uses a German non-finite construction that results in an additional clause in (19):

(18)   a.   *[One of President Bush's primary objectives in that meeting was] [to take a further step in our efforts] [to persuade President Putin] [to join us in] [creating a new strategic framework for] [dealing with the security threats] [that we now face,] [while moving us toward a cooperative relationship with Russia and away from the adversarial legacy of the Cold War.]* (EO_SPEECH_003)

   b.   *[Eines der vorrangigen Ziele von Präsident Bush bei diesem Treffen war es,] [einen Schritt voranzukommen bei unseren Bemühungen,] [Präsident Putin zu überzeugen,] [mit uns gemeinsam einen neuen strategischen Rahmen für die Handhabung von Sicherheitsbedrohungen zu schaffen,] [denen wir uns nun gegenübersehen,] [während wir gleichzeitig auf kooperative Beziehungen zu Russland hinarbeiten] [und die feindliche Gesinnung des Kalten Kriegs hinter uns lassen.]* (GTrans_SPEECH_003)

Here, it is semantically impossible to retain the structure *moving us toward ...and away from* in the translation. Two different verbs have to be used and thus one clause in the English text is split into two clauses in the German translation.

(19)   a. *[Our European friends and allies share our concern about the need] [to accord recognition to surviving Holocaust victims within their lifetimes.]* (EO_SPEECH_006)

       b. *[Unsere europäischen Freunde und Bündnispartner teilen unser Anliegen,] [den überlebenden Holocaust-Opfern zu Lebzeiten Anerkennung zuteil werden] [zu lassen.]* (GTrans_SPEECH_006)

In (19), the translator uses an infinitive construction with the modifying verb *lassen*, which leads to two verbs and therefore two clauses, where the English original formulation consists of only one clause.

Apart from these few cases, the German translations adhere rather closely to the English source texts. 94.04% of the clauses are aligned, and it seems as if the translators are trying to use the same structures in the German texts that can be found in the English ones. This could be interpreted as source language shining through, which is, as it were, the 'counterpart' of normalization. Lexico-grammatical properties of the source language can be reflected in the target language as well, especially in areas where the target language is more flexible than the source language (Teich 2003: 218). With regard to pre- and postmodification it is therefore possible that the German translations follow the pattern used in the English originals, because German is not confined to one specific option, but can afford to more or less copy the structures of the English text. This strategy would result in a lower number of empty links.

Nevertheless, it has to be borne in mind that there are also empty links in the English source texts. They occur, for example, where English non-finite constructions are translated with the help of nominal constructions, as can be seen in example (20).

(20)   a. *[As a result: in the Middle East, countries are going back to the negotiating table,] [we have established a new relationship with Russia] [that promises] [to form the a [sic] new framework of constructive arms control agreements,] [and we are openly discussing the very real problems and the hard reality] [attached to the proliferation of weapons of mass destruction.]* (EO_SPEECH_005)

       b. *[Das Ergebnis hiervon ist: – die Rückkehr der Länder im Nahen Osten an den Verhandlungstisch, – der Aufbau neuer Beziehungen zu*

Russland, [die das Versprechen eines neuen Rahmens für konstruktive Rüstungskontrollabkommen bergen,] und – eine offene Diskussion über die sehr realen Probleme und die harsche Wirklichkeit im Zusammenhang mit der Verbreitung von Massenvernichtungswaffen.]
(GTrans_SPEECH_005)

The results of US President Bush's policies are listed with bullet points in the English source text. For each result the author starts with a new sentence, sometimes containing several clauses. In the German translation, each result is presented as a noun phrase containing no verbs. As explained above, this rather dense discourse information structure is characteristic of German.

Empty links at clause level can be attributed in most cases to contrastive differences between English and German. In terms of translation properties, these differences often result in explicitation (mainly in the English translations) and normalization in combination with source language shining through, as a closer look at the high number of empty links in the English texts reveals. The combination of source language shining through and target language normalization leads to a hybridization in the translations.

4.3 Crossing lines between words and grammatical functions

Crossing lines between words and grammatical functions shed light on the variation in terms of grammatical "responsibility" of the words used in the parallel versions.[8] They are thus indicative of shifts in perspective as, for instance, described by Vinay & Darbelnet (1958) in terms of modulation, i.e. a semantic shift in perspective.

As mentioned previously, the validity of the query results for crossing lines on all levels involving word level is limited due to the relatively low quality of the existing word alignment (especially concerning recall; see also §3.3). In terms of the present discussion this means that we can only draw some very preliminary conclusions from the existing figures. A cursory look at the aligned texts suggests that there are frequent candidates for crossing lines that are not retrieved by our query because the recall of our word alignment tools is still lower than one would wish.

---

[8] The percentage of crossing lines for words and grammatical functions is calculated on the basis of the number amount of grammatical functions (per subcorpus) for which word shifts occur (the percentage of sentences containing crossing lines between words and grammatical functions in relation to the number of all sentences per register.).

Figure 4 shows that crossing lines are similarly frequent in pairs of source and target registers. The clearest pattern emerging is an organization in registers. All SHARE subcorpora display a similarly high frequency of crossing lines, just as all FICTION subcorpora display a comparably low frequency of crossing lines. The only register not showing such a clear pattern is SPEECH. Here, the pairs of original and target registers are still grouped together. This becomes particularly obvious when only taking into account lexical words and excluding function words as depicted in Figure 4.

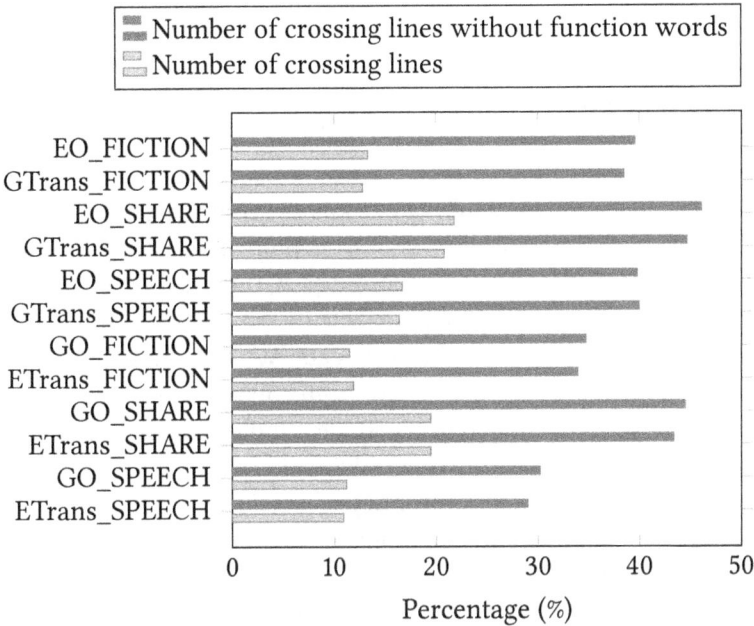

Figure 4: Percentages of crossing lines between words and grammatical functions

This raises the question of why it is this level that appears to be prone to register influences. One starting point could be differing distributions of grammatical functions in the registers. If the grammatical functions are distributed differently in the four subcorpora in one register, this could be reflected in more crossing lines between originals and translations in this register. In order to assess the variation between subcorpora in the three registers, we compute the standard deviation between the values for each function in the individual registers. The sum of the individual standard deviations should be higher in a register containing more variation between the functions. As Table 3 shows, SHARE in fact has more variation reflected by higher standard deviations for the individual functions. The lowest variation is found in FICTION, which has consistently lower frequencies of crossing lines.

While this appears to be a plausible explanation for the differing numbers of crossing lines, contrastive differences, i.e. an aspect not related to the register, could play a role as well. Prepositional objects and complements, for instance, display different frequencies in the two languages resulting in more similarities between originals and translations in the same language (see Table 3). Apparently, prepositional objects play a greater role in the German registers whereas complements appear to be more typical of the English registers. Consequently, it is these functions in particular that seem to be more prone to crossing lines.

Table 4 displays the most frequent crossing lines between words and grammatical functions organized by register and translation direction. Due to the abovementioned weaknesses of recall in our word alignment, we do not interpret frequencies but only the ranking of the most common shifts.

Table 4 shows how the translators shift from prepositional object to other functions in the translation direction German-English, thus adapting to the target language preferences, e.g. prepositional objects in the German FICTION texts are frequently translated by English direct objects. When translating from English to German, translators shift words away from complements to other functions, e.g. in SHARE to prepositional objects. Table 4 indicates that this also works in the opposite direction: translators not only avoid functions that are less typical in the target language, but also shift into preferred functions. Words are moved from various German functions into English complements, as exemplified by the second to fourth rank in SPEECH translations into English in Table 4. A shift from German prepositional objects to English direct objects may be a general strategy not necessarily limited to a given register, as shown by the fact that this crossing line is most common in registers as divergent as FICTION and SHARE and is still fairly common in SPEECH. Examples (21) to (24) exemplify these shifts for the three registers.

(21)   a. *Er hat sich darauf verlassen, dass wir von drinnen sein Lächeln sehen*
         können. (GO_FICTION_007)

       b. *He just assumed we could see his smile from inside.*
         (ETrans_FICTION_007)

Together with and initiated by the pronominal adverb *darauf,* the whole *dass* subordinate clause in the German original in (21) forms a prepositional object. Note that the annotation on which this discussion is based is limited to the

Table 3: Distribution of grammatical functions per subcorpus in percent

	EO	ETrans	GO	GTrans	Std. dev.
FICTION					
ADV_*	18.87	18.01	18.40	19.94	0.8335
APPO	0.92	0.68	0.71	0.70	0.1141
COMPL	5.19	5.04	3.78	3.28	0.9389
DOBJ	10.77	10.26	10.82	11.76	0.6262
FIN	23.43	23.20	24.39	23.87	0.5243
IOBJ	0.81	0.81	1.93	2.03	0.6766
other	6.76	7.61	7.75	7.09	0.4581
PRED	6.04	6.75	4.83	5.26	0.8515
PROBJ	1.74	1.75	2.49	2.27	0.3765
SUBJ	21.08	21.27	19.86	19.37	0.9263
SHARE					
ADV_*	17.98	18.22	21.15	21.28	1.8005
APPO	1.60	1.15	0.41	0.81	0.5065
COMPL	6.42	6.54	4.16	4.15	1.3433
DOBJ	12.19	10.73	10.47	11.54	0.7870
FIN	22.54	21.75	20.96	21.33	0.6771
IOBJ	0.88	0.93	1.70	1.54	0.4196
other	11.07	12.10	12.64	11.50	0.6863
PRED	7.22	9.12	8.87	8.27	0.8487
PROBJ	2.84	2.62	4.40	4.68	1.0562
SUBJ	21.32	20.82	19.78	19.17	0.9756
SPEECH					
ADV_*	14.61	15.52	16.91	15.90	0.9534
APPO	0.81	1.41	0.83	0.42	0.4117
COMPL	6.06	8.06	5.79	5.57	1.1422
DOBJ	12.18	10.35	10.92	12.70	1.0893
FIN	22.63	21.86	21.41	22.95	0.7017
IOBJ	0.76	0.49	1.82	1.62	0.6467
OTHER	6.79	7.96	9.05	6.30	1.2312
PRED	11.08	10.21	8.27	8.92	1.2644
PROBJ	2.93	2.21	3.94	4.25	0.9357
SUBJ	22.05	21.85	21.00	21.24	0.4977

Table 4: The ten most frequent crossing lines per register and translation direction

FICTION		SHARE		SPEECH	
E2G	G2E	E2G	G2E	E2G	G2E
dobj → subj	probj → dobj	compl → probj	probj → dobj	dobj → probj	subj → dobj
compl → dobj	dobj → subj	dobj → subj	subj → compl	dobj → compl	subj → compl
subj → dobj	fin → pred	dobj → probj	subj → dobj	compl → probj	probj → compl
dobj → fin	compl → subj	compl → dobj	probj → compl	subj → dobj	dobj → compl
dobj → probj	subj → dobj	dobj → compl	dobj → compl	dobj → subj	probj → dobj
fin → dobj	dobj → compl	compl → subj	fin → pred	pred → fin	dobj → subj
adv_mod → dobj	fin → compl	probj → dobj	dobj → subj	compl → dobj	fin → compl
pred → fin	pred → fin	subj → dobj	compl → dobj	compl → subj	fin → pred
compl → subj	fin → subj	fin → pred	adv_mod → compl	subj → compl	fin → subj
adv_cause → dobj	fin → dobj	pred → fin	subj → probj	compl → fin	compl → subj

highest node in the sentence, thus the *dass* clause is not analyzed further. This discontinuous prepositional object is shifted to a direct object in the English translation. In our query, the hit for the shift is triggered by the aligned noun pair *Lächeln* in the German prepositional object and *smile* in the English direct object. However, this analysis is somewhat problematic. Taking a closer look, we can see that *Lächeln* is actually part of a direct object in the *dass* clause, and should not account for the shift from prepositional object to the direct object. This effect is due to our top-level only annotation, an issue we will come back to in §5.2.

(22) a. *1995 haben wir auf 125 Jahre Deutsche Bank zurückgeblickt.*
      (GO_SHARE_009)

      b. *In 1995 we celebrated Deutsche Bank's 125th anniversary.*
      (ETrans_SHARE_009)

In (22) from the SHARE register, the name of the bank reporting to its shareholders is shifted from the postmodification within the prepositional object in German to premodification of the direct object in the English translation.

(23) a. *Nach wie vor ist der Zinsüberschuß nach Risikovorsorge mit 9,7 Mrd DM die bei weitem wichtigste Ertragskomponente. Allerdings weisen die unterschiedlichen Steigerungsraten der einzelnen Ergebniskomponenten auf die Veränderungen im Geschäft hin.* (GO_SHARE_009)

      b. *Although net interest income after provision for losses on loans and advances, at DM 9.7 billion, is still by far the most important component of income, the individual figures highlight the changes in our business.* (ETrans_SHARE_009)

(24) a. *Daher setzen wir uns nachdrücklich für die Schaffung eines*
          europäischen Systems der Finanzaufsicht ein. (GO_SPEECH_002)

     b. *Hence we expressly support the establishment of a European system of*
          financial supervision. (ETrans_SPEECH_002)

Example (23) still from SHARE and (24) from SPEECH underline that the specific type of crossing lines exemplified there is largely due to lexical reasons. The German verb *hinweisen* selects the preposition *auf* for its object. Possibly, this finding points to a higher frequency of verbs taking certain types of prepositional object in German than in English. Globally, however, this has to be related to phrasal verbs whose particle is annotated as part of the verb in the CroCo annotation and consequently only leaving prepositional verbs as those taking a prepositional object.

Other shifts may be more restricted to a given register, as, for instance, the shift from an English complement to a German prepositional object. This is particularly prominent in SHARE. Here, often similar reasons apply as with empty links for complements described in §4.1.

Having established some potential causes for individual phenomena in the three registers, we can now return to the overall number of crossing lines on this level in the three registers. Compared to the other two registers under scrutiny here, the figures suggest that FICTION has relatively few crossing lines in both translation directions (see Figure 4). Frequently, crossing lines concern changes between finite and predicator, as is the case in example (23). The perfect tense in the English original is translated by a present tense verb in German, thus resulting in a crossing line of *happened* and *geschieht*.

(25) a. *And what has happened before a few years have passed?*
          (EO_FICTION_006)

     b. *Und was geschieht, ehe noch ein paar Jahre vergangen sind?*
          (GTrans_FICTION_006)

While the shift in (25) can be attributed to a deliberate change in tense by the translator, the shift between finite and predicator in (26) is due to language contrast.

(26) a. *Aber Sie wissen nichts.* (GO_FICTION_007)

     b. *But you don't know anything.* (ETrans_FICTION_007)

The English negation requires the auxiliary *do* that results in the dissociation of the predicate into the finite auxiliary and the full verb as predicator. The German text does not require this and consequently only consists of a finite.

An informationally more marked use of German as in (27) results in a frequent crossing line in this register and translation direction, a shift between direct object and subject.

(27)   a. *Die Frauen hat das nicht gerade zimperlich gemacht.*
          (GO_FICTION_007)

      b. *The women weren't exactly prudes.* (ETrans_FICTION_007)

The translator has avoided putting the direct object at the front of the sentence in the English translation, as is the case in the German original. For English, this order of grammatical functions is highly marked. Preserving the order of the content, the translator here decided to shift *women* to the subject function, adhering to the more rigid canonical order of grammatical functions in English, thus of course sacrificing some of the information structure of the original.

SPEECH contains the lowest number of crossing lines in the translation direction German to English. Even fairly complex structures as in (28) do not necessarily require numerous shifts in grammatical functions.

(28)   a. *Wenn wir also in diesem Sinne unseren Interessen und Werten dienen*
          wollen, dann muss Europa erstens wachsam gegenüber den neuen
          Bedrohungen sein, denen die freien und offenen Gesellschaften
          ausgesetzt sind. (GO_SPEECH_010)

      b. *So if we want to serve our interests and values in line with this*
          definition, Europe must: firstly, be vigilant to the new threats to which
          the free and open societies are exposed. (ETrans_SPEECH 010)

Possibly, this is due to a more canonical word order in the German SPEECH register requiring fewer adjustments in the English translation to conform to the more fixed word order of English. The percentage of subjects in sentence-initial position appears to corroborate this assumption. The percentages of grammatical subjects in relation to all grammatical functions in sentence-initial position in the German FICTION and SHARE registers are 42.16% and 45.87% respectively. By contrast, SPEECH exhibits 54.45% of subjects in this position, displaying a register-specific feature and thus making the English translators' task easier.

In the opposite translation direction, SPEECH contains more crossing lines between words and grammatical functions. A potential language contrast between English and German is a shift from coordination to subordination as in

(29). This is reflected in crossing lines because the whole subordinate clause in the translation is analyzed as one grammatical function in the CroCo annotation (here an adverbial) whereas the chunks in the coordinated clause are analyzed individually (*resolution* is part of a direct object).

(29)   a. *Every country has its own political issues and this makes resolution of our disputes increasingly difficult.* (EO_SPEECH_009)

   b. *Jedes Land hat seine eigenen politischen Anliegen, wodurch die Streitschlichtung zunehmend erschwert wird.* (GTrans_SPEECH_009)

Example (30) displays a shift where the word *fight* is moved from the direct object in the original to the subject in the German translation. This represents a typical case of modulation, where the perspective is shifted from the persons confronted with this fight to the fight itself. Beyond the translation shift of modulation this exemplifies House's (1997) cross-cultural difference in terms of orientation towards persons in English versus orientation towards content in German.

(30)   a. *And if the EU does as it has in the past, and provides financing to Airbus at below- market rates of return, we could be facing a very large and highly contentious fight in the WTO.* (EO_SPEECH_009)

   b. *Und wenn die EU sich wie in der Vergangenheit verhält und dem Airbus Finanzierung zu Zinssätzen unter den auf dem Markt gültigen bietet, könnte uns ein großer und sehr kontroverser Kampf in der WTO bevorstehen.* (GTrans_SPEECH_009)

Word order contrasts combined with different mappings of semantic roles onto grammatical functions between English and German may typically result in crossing lines as represented by (31). The subject of the German passive original is positioned after the finite, which does not lead to an informationally highly marked construction in German. Rather than rearranging the linear precedence of clause elements in English, the translator has opted for rearranging the assignment of semantic roles to grammatical functions by choosing active voice. *Basis*, the aligned translation of *Grundlage*, is consequently no longer part of the subject but of the direct object. Example (32) displays a similar case.

(31)   a. *Gleichzeitig wurde hiermit auch die Grundlage für die Einführung von Hedgefonds in Deutschland und damit für den direkten Zugang deutscher Anleger zu diesem innovativen Produkt gelegt.* (GO_SPEECH_002)

b. *At the same time it established the basis for the introduction of hedge funds in, thus affording German investors direct access to this innovative product.* (ETrans_SPEECH_002)

(32) a. *Damit werden Investitionen von rund 10 Mrd. DM angestoßen und 5–7 Mio. t CO2 eingespart.* (GO_SPEECH_001)

b. *It will generate investments of around 10 billion marks and reduce CO2 emissions by 5–7 million metric tons.* (ETrans_SPEECH_001)

Examples (33) and (34) represent cases where there is no apparent reason forcing the translator to change the word order and, at the same time, the voice of the sentence. The crossing lines can be seen as symptoms of a whole range of changes that are obviously due to the translator. When seen in combination with the respective source sentence, these translations show clear indications of the translation process as a motivating variable. Nevertheless, they do not easily lend themselves to an interpretation in terms of translation properties as described by Baker (1996) and others.

(33) a. *In Deutschland haben wir bisher noch keine Entscheidung über die Einführung von REITs getroffen.* (GO_SPEECH_002)

b. *No decision has yet been taken in Germany on the introduction of REITs.* (ETrans_SPEECH_002)

(34) a. *Dieser Markt hat sein Potenzial bei weitem noch nicht ausgeschöpft.* (GO_SPEECH_002)

b. *The full potential of this market is by no means exhausted.* (ETrans_SPEECH_002)

Concentrating on SHARE, where most of the crossing lines occur in both directions, we find examples like (35). Here, a different constituent structure (subject complement plus complementation in EO versus full verb plus prepositional object in GTrans) mapped onto very similar structures in terms of word order results in a crossing line. A certain share of instances of crossing lines can be analyzed in the same way. Example (36), however, is more representative of shifts occurring in translation in our data. Whereas *Der Wandel* (*the change*) constitutes the subject in the German original, it is realized as a prepositional object in the translation with the patient becoming the subject. This results in a major shift in perspective in the translation.

(35) a. *The same is true for Human Resources reviews.* (EO_SHARE_004)

  b. *Das gleiche gilt für "Human Resources Reviews".* (GTrans_SHARE_004)

(36) a. *Der Wandel geht an unseren Filialen nicht vorüber.* (GO_SHARE_009)

  b. *Our branches are not unaffected by these changes.*
      (ETrans_SHARE_009)

The crossing line in example (37) is equally interesting in that, among a number of shifts, the subject of the original (*die moderne Universalbank*) is hidden in the postmodification of the complement in the translation (*an impressive demonstration of a modern universal bank's capabilities*).

(37) a. *Mit ihrer Plazierungskraft im Inland hat die moderne Universalbank ihre Möglichkeiten eindrucksvoll unterstrichen.* (GO_SHARE_009)

  b. *The placement of this issue in Germany was an impressive demonstration of a modern universal bank's capabilities.*
      (ETrans_SHARE_009)

Beyond modulation as a type of translation shift these crossing lines do not easily lend themselves to interpretations in terms of translation properties. Instances like (37) point to implicitation rather than explicitation in terms of constituency structure, because the referent (and the words) contained in the subject in the original is not only shifted into the complement in the translation, but is additionally reduced to postmodification instead of representing the head of the phrase in the original.

The discussion of crossing lines between words and grammatical functions has shown that these crossing lines are symptomatic of a whole range of factors relevant to translation. Of course they are subject to a wide range of influences that prohibit mono-causal explanations. They are, however, indicative of differences between registers as well as contrastive differences in the frequency of certain grammatical functions and in word order. Furthermore, they show translation shifts, typically in the area of modulation, which must often be attributed to translator behavior. Finally, we have also shown dimensions of cross-cultural differences in House's sense at work.

A direct and simplistic association between crossing lines between words and grammatical functions and translation properties should be avoided: while crossing lines definitely have implications for properties such as explicitation, normalization, simplification, shining through and others, the relationship is complex and needs further evidence.

5 Future work

We have shown in this paper the query power which can be provided by an annotation which comprises multi-level annotation and alignment and which to a considerable extent can be done (semi-)automatically, at least when it comes to tagging and chunking. The value of the CroCo-specific annotation lies on the one hand in the alignment which was partly done by human annotators (for the clause and sentence level). On the other hand, the manual annotation of levels like phrase structure and grammatical functions delivers a high-quality set of data. Moreover, we have demonstrated the methodological value of querying empty links and crossing lines for the detection of translation shifts and investigation of translation properties. Within the context of the CroCo project there are a number of spin-off projects, e.g. further investigating cohesion in originals and translations, or how "parallel" valency is between English and German. In some of these projects, the limitations of the CroCo annotation – esp. the decision to keep the functional annotation on the top level, with the exception of clauses which are annotated for their functions as well – become obvious.

In §5.1 we outline some thoughts on how the findings in this paper will help realize a project on valency queries. In order to study valency and other phenomena in a more detailed fashion and on all linguistic levels, i.e. with respect not just to main and subordinate clauses, but also to embedded structures, we will add deeper annotation levels to CroCo. We briefly sketch out these plans in §5.2.

5.1 Valency queries

One of the big hopes in parallel corpora is that they may enable us to build multilingual valency dictionaries (semi-)automatically. This would facilitate the work of the lexicographer enormously. Corpora allow for the extraction of large amounts of data in a short time and may contain examples a lexicographer would not easily think of. Examples for monolingual valency dictionaries based on corpora are the Czech PDT-VALLEX[9] and the English Erlangen Valency Pattern Bank.[10]

In order for valency queries to work, we must rely on the fact that the structures are maximally equivalent between original and translation. As we have seen in our results, this is more valid for some linguistic levels than for others. For the sentence level, for instance, we found that in all registers and all translation directions at least 99% of the sentences have an equivalent. If we see the

---

[9] http://ufal.mff.cuni.cz/vallex/2.5/doc/home.html

[10] http://www.patternbank.uni-erlangen.de/cgi-bin/patternbank.cgi

sentence as a valency carrier plus the complements and adjuncts accompanying it, this means for the purpose of valency extraction that in 99% of all cases we will have a pair of structures which can be used for further investigation.

The results on empty links and crossing lines for grammatical functions, which we presented in this paper, will be most valuable for our valency studies as well. The considerable number of occurrences for these two phenomena already suggest that we are likely to find quite a number of valency-related phenomena which occur in translation. In example (14), for instance, we have a case in which the nominal group *zur Sicherung von Beschäftigung* was translated with a verbal expression *to safeguarding jobs*, resulting in an empty link on the clause level. From a valency point of view, the shift from noun to verb also shifts the syntactic valency frame of *Sicherung* which adds the object as a *von*-PP, compared to the direct object *jobs* that the verbal equivalent *safeguarding* requires. Another kind of valency shift involves cases of shifts in grammatical functions, which have been described in §4.3. Furthermore, a pilot study has revealed that there is a considerable percentage of cases in which the main verbs do not perfectly match. This was the case for about 20-40% in our sample of 300 sentence pairs (50 from each register and translation direction). For the instances of divergences found, there was either a shift in meaning (e.g. *jmdm. gut tun* 'do so. good' vs. *benefit from sth.*) or the full verb on the one side has a syntactically more complex equivalent on the other side, e.g. a copula construction, an idiomatic expression or a support verb construction, often changing the overall structure of the sentence. As for copula constructions, it has already been outlined in §4.1 that they are more frequent in English and thus account for quite a number of empty links for shifts departing from (predicative) complements. There seems to be only a small minority of cases in which a sentence has been completely re-phrased, thus rendering the sentence pair useless for the study of valency-related phenomena.

In order to study these phenomena, we will need a deeper annotation of structures, which will be provided by converting (parts of) the CroCo corpus to a parallel dependency treebank, the plans for which are briefly outlined in the following subsection.

5.2 Towards a parallel treebank

Let us go back to our *Lächeln*-example (21) from §4.3. We can see in this example, as has already been discussed in §4.3, that the top-level-only annotation in CroCo sometimes negatively affects our queries. The *dass*-clause is combined into a prepositional object together with the *darauf*-adverb. When querying for the word pair *Lächeln* and *smile*, we get a shift from prepositional object to direct object, which is triggered by our method of analyzing the structure rather than a real shift. This kind of annotation is also disadvantageous when looking into valency phenomena. Elements might be deeper embedded when shifting from full verb to copula plus adjective-constructions, for instance. We would like to be able to detect these kinds of shifts automatically as well.

We have thus decided to transform at least parts of the CroCo-annotation into a parallel dependency treebank, in a spin-off project. When tentatively translating our functional analysis of the German original sentence from the *Lächeln*-example into a dependency tree, we could get an analysis as exemplified in Figure 5. From a dependency tree like that depicted in the figure, we can deduce the correct grammatical function for *Lächeln*, but still preserve the information that the whole subordinate clause with *sehen* as root functions as a prepositional object.

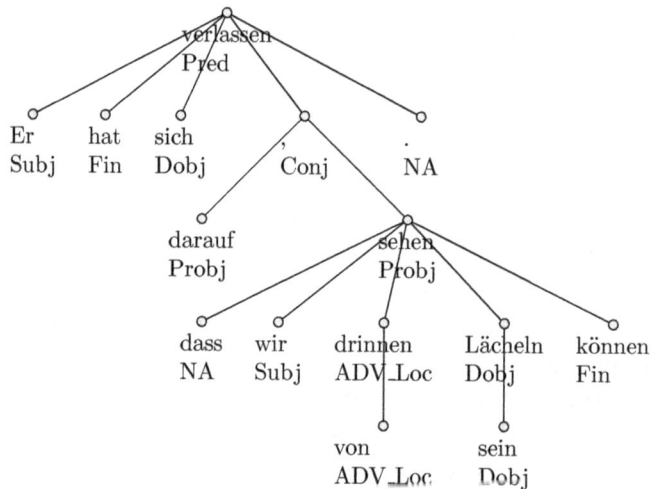

Figure 5: A possible dependency analysis for example (21a)

We will be using the tools created within the Prague Dependency Treebank project, namely TrEd[11] plus some extensions for working with parallel data which it delivers (Böhmova et al. 2000). We will annotate dependencies at the functional level, using grammatical categories such as subject, object etc. Annotation of deep syntactic or semantic roles is not planned at present, but may be added at a later stage. The trees will be aligned on the level of the grammatical functions. This alignment will allow us to more reliably query shifts on this level.

---

[11] http://ufal.mff.cuni.cz/~pajas/tred/

References

Baker, Mona. 1993. Corpus linguistics and translation studies: Implications and applications. In Mona Baker, Gill Francis & Elena Tognini-Bonelli (eds.), *Text and technology: In honour of John Sinclair*, 233–250. Amsterdam & Philadelphia: John Benjamins.

Baker, Mona. 1995. Corpora in translation studies: An overview and some suggestions for future research. *Target* 7(2). 223–243.

Baker, Mona. 1996. Corpus-based translation studies: The challenges that lie ahead. In Harold Somers (ed.), *Terminology, LSP and translation. Studies in language engineering in honour of Juan C. Sager*, 175–186. Amsterdam: John Benjamins.

Blum-Kulka, Shoshana. 1986. Shifts of cohesion and coherence in translation. In Juliane House & Shoshana Blum-Kulka (eds.), *Interlingual and intercultural communication: Discourse and cognition in translation and second language acquisition studies*, 17–35. Tübingen: Gunter Narr.

Brants, Thorsten. 2000. TnT: A statistical part-of-speech tagger. In *Proceedings of the Sixth Conference on Applied Natural Language Processing*, 224–231.

Bresnan, Joan & Ronald Kaplan. 1982. Lexical-functional grammar: A formal system for grammatical representation. In Joan Bresnan (ed.), *The mental representation of grammatical relations*, 173–281. Cambridge: MIT Press.

Burnard, Lou & Syd Bauman. 2007. *TEI P5: Guidelines for electronic text encoding and interchange.* Text Encoding Initiative.

Böhmova, Alena, Jan Hajič, Eva Hajičová & Barbora Hladká. 2000. The Prague Dependency Treebank: A three-level annotation scenario. In Anne Abeillé (ed.), *Treebanks: Building and using syntactically annotated corpora.* Dordrecht: Kluwer Academic.

Catford, John C. 1965. *A linguistic theory of translation: An essay in applied linguistics.* Oxford: Oxford University Press.

Čulo, Oliver, Silvia Hansen-Schirra, Stella Neumann & Mihaela Vela. 2008. Empirical studies on language contrast using the English-German comparable and parallel CroCo Corpus. In *Proceedings of the LREC 2008 Workshop "Building and using comparable corpora", Marrakesh, Morrocco, 31 May 2008*, 47–51. Marrakesh.

Cyrus, Lea. 2006. Building a resource for studying translation shifts. In *Proceedings of LREC-2006*, 1240–1245. Genoa.

Fabricius-Hansen, Catherine. 1998. Informational density and translation, with special reference to German – Norwegian – English. In Stig Johansson & Signe

Oksefjell (eds.), *Corpora and cross-linguistic research. Theory, method and case studies*, 197–234. Amsterdam & Atlanta: Rodopi.

Gurevych, Iryna, Max Mühlhäuser, Christof Müller, Jürgen Steimle, Markus Weimer & Torsten Zesch. 2007. Darmstadt knowledge processing repository based on UIMA. In *Proceedings of the first Workshop on Unstructured Information Management Architecture at Biannual Conference of the Society for Computational Linguistics and Language Technology*. Tübingen.

Halliday, M. A. K. 1985. *An introduction to Functional Grammar*. London: Arnold.

Hansen-Schirra, Silvia, Stella Neumann & Erich Steiner. 2007. Cohesive explicitness and explicitation in an English-German translation corpus. *Languages in Contrast* 7(2). 241–265.

Hansen-Schirra, Silvia, Stella Neumann & Erich Steiner. 2012a. *Cross-linguistic corpora for the study of translations – Insights from the language pair English-German*. Berlin: de Gruyter.

Hansen-Schirra, Silvia, Stella Neumann & Erich Steiner. 2012b. *Cross-linguistic corpora for the study of translations: Insights from the language pair English-German*. Berlin: de Gruyter.

Hansen-Schirra, Silvia, Stella Neumann & Michaela Vela. 2006. Multidimensional annotation and alignment in an English-German translation corpus. In *Proceedings of the 5th Workshop on NLP and XML (NLPXML-2006): Multi-Dimensional Markup in Natural Language Processing*, 35–42. Trento: ACL.

Hawkins, John A. 1986. *A comparative typology of English and German: Unifying the contrasts*. London: Croom Helm.

Heyn, Matthias. 1996. Integrating machine translation into translation memory systems. In *European association for machine translation. Workshop proceedings*.

House, Juliane. 1997. *Translation quality assessment: A model revisited*. Tübingen: Gunter Narr.

Koller, Werner. 2001. *Einführung in die Übersetzungswissenschaft*. Tübingen: Gunter Narr.

Leuven-Zwart, van Kitty. 1989. Translation and original: Similarities and dissimilarities. *Target* 1(2). 151–181.

Maas, Heinz Dieter, Christoph Rösener & Axel Theofilidis. 2009. Morphosyntactic and semantic analysis of text: The MPRO tagging procedure. In Cerstin Mahlow & Michael Piotrowski (eds.), *State of the art in computational morphology. Workshop on Systems and Frameworks for Computational Morphology 2009*, 76–87. New York: Springer.

Müller, Cornelia & Michael Strube. 2006. Multi-level annotation of linguistic data with MMAX2. In Sabine Braun, Kurt Kohn & Joybrato Mukherjee (eds.), *Corpus technology and language pedagogy: New ressources, new tools, new methods*, 197–214. Frankfurt a. M.: Peter Lang.

Neumann, Stella. 2014. *Contrastive register variation: A quantitative approach to the comparison of English and German*. Berlin PhD thesis.

Newmark, Peter. 1988. *A textbook of translation*. New York: Prentice Hall.

Och, Franz-Josef & Hermann Ney. 2003. A systematic comparison of various statistical alignment models. *Computational Linguistics* 29(1). 19–51.

Özgür, Dindar. 2007. *TIGER API 1.8: A Java interface to the TIGER corpus*. http://www.tigerapi.org.

Padó, Sebastian. 2007. Translational equivalence and cross-lingual parallelism: The case of framenet frames. In *Proceedings of the nodalida workshop on building frame semantics resources for scandinavian and baltic languages*. Tartu.

Pollard, Carl & Ivan A. Sag. 1994. *Head-driven phrase structure grammar*. Chicago: University of Chicago Press.

Sampson, Geoffrey. 1995. *English for the computer: The Susanne Corpus and analytic scheme*. Oxford: Clarendon Press.

Schiller, Anne, Simone Teufel, Christine Stöckert & Christine Thielen. 1999. *Guidelines für das Tagging deutscher Textcorpora mit STTS*. Universität Stuttgart, Universität Tübingen.

Sperberg-McQueen, C. Michael & Lou Burnard (eds.). 1994. *Guidelines for electronic text encoding and interchange (TEI P3)*. Chicago & Oxford: Text Encoding Initiative.

Steiner, Erich. 2008. Empirical studies of translations as a mode of language contact: "explicitness" of lexicogrammatical encoding as a relevant dimension. In Peter Siemund & Noemi Kintana (eds.), *Language contact and contact languages*, 317–346. Amsterdam: John Benjamins.

Teich, Elke. 2003. *Cross-linguistic variation in system and text: A methodology for the investigation of translations and comparable texts*. Berlin & New York: Mouton de Gruyter.

Toury, Gideon. 1995. *Descriptive translation studies and beyond*. Amsterdam & Philadelphia: John Benjamins.

Vinay, Jean-Paul & Jean Darbelnet. 1958. *Stylistique comparée du français et de l'anglais: Méthode de traduction*. Paris: Didier.

Chapter 5

On drafting and revision in translation: A corpus linguistics oriented analysis of translation process data

Fabio Alves
Federal University of Minas Gerais

Daniel Couto Vale
Federal University of Minas Gerais

This chapter reports on a study which investigates prototypical characteristics of the drafting and revision phases of the translation process, mapped onto the sequential unfolding of micro translation units into macro translation units (MTUs). By using LITTERAE, an annotation and search tool designed to mark, annotate and extract XML files of key-logged translation process data, the chapter analyses the performance of 12 professional translators and classifies their output as MTUs grouped into three categories: MTUs containing micro units which are processed solely during the drafting phase (P1 type), MTUs containing micro units which are processed once in the drafting phase and finalised in the revision phase (P2 type), and MTUs containing micro units which are processed during the drafting phase and taken up again during the revision phase (P3 type). The analysis points to a hierarchical structure in which P1 is more predominant than P2 which, in turn, is more frequent than P3.

1 Introduction

Corpus linguistics tools have been applied to research in translation studies to analyse large amounts of translated texts aiming at identifying prototypical translation patterns (Olohan & Baker 2000; Hansen-Schirra, Neumann & Steiner 2007, among others). Although insightful, the results of these studies do not provide explanation for those intermediate solutions which are deleted in the course of text production and do not surface in the target texts. Drawing on a different approach, translation process research has a long-standing tradition of trying to ac-

Fabio Alves & Daniel Couto Vale. 2017. On drafting and revision in translation: A corpus linguistics oriented analysis of translation process data. In Silvia Hansen-Schirra, Stella Neumann & Oliver Čulo (eds.), *Annotation, exploitation and evaluation of parallel corpora*, 89–110. Berlin: Language Science Press. DOI:10.5281/zenodo.283500

count for these interim versions which occur in the different phases of the translation process (Alves 2007). However, research on translation process data from the perspective of corpus linguistics is still quite incipient. CORPRAT, the Corpus on Process for the Analysis of Translations, developed by LETRA, the Laboratory for Experimentation in Translation (Pagano, Magalhães & Alves 2004) is perhaps the first attempt to apply a corpus linguistics oriented approach to the analysis of translation process data. Until last year CORPRAT only stored and retrieved translation process data for research purposes. Lately, with the advent of the LIT-TERAE search tool (Alves & Vale 2009), it became possible not only to store and retrieve translation process data in CORPRAT but also to mark, annotate and extract translation process data using corpus linguistics tools. Thus, it is now possible to query large amounts of translation process data semi-automatically, to identify prototypical patterns of online text production in translation, and to assess its unfolding in terms of sequential steps which can provide insights into instances of cognitive planning and cognitive effort in translation.

This chapter looks at prototypical traits of drafting and revision patterns from a process-oriented perspective. To do so, it analyses translations carried out by 12 professional translators – six translating from English into Brazilian Portuguese and six translating from German into Brazilian Portuguese. The aim of the chapter is to examine the unfolding of micro translation units into macro translation units (Alves & Vale 2009; Alves et al. 2010) and to describe which patterns can be ascribed prototypically to particular phases of the translation process. It also sheds light onto hierarchical patterns which can be seen as indicative of prototypical characteristics observed in different stages of the translation process.

2 Theoretical underpinnings

2.1 Development of CORPRAT

Pagano, Magalhães & Alves (2004) describe the rationale for the design of COR-PRAT, the Corpus on Process for the Analysis of Translations. The database has been designed to store larger sets of data related to the process of on-line text production in translation. Over the past few years, the amount of data stored in it has been expanded significantly. CORPRAT aims at providing further insights into the translation process, raising new hypotheses and presenting more robust evidence to support or refute general claims about the translation process.

Building on research that favours a small corpora approach (Ghadessy & Gao 2001) to corpus linguistics, CORPRAT stores five complementary kinds of files generated through key logging, screen recording, eye tracking, recordings/transcriptions of retrospective protocols and questionnaires, allowing inquiries of translation process data from different perspectives. CORPRAT data also allows target text (TT) production to be examined as finished end products or as interim versions portraying intermediate stages of target text production such as the ones produced during or at the end of the drafting phase as well as during and at the end of the revision phase (Jakobsen 2002).

The language pairs available in CORPRAT comprise Brazilian Portuguese and either English, German or Spanish. Data from experimental research stored in the corpus reflect the performance of subjects who vary from novice to expert translators, and also include subject-domain experts who are not translators (Pagano & Silva 2008). The combined files in CORPRAT are used to account for particular traits and features in translation processes, including research on the acquisition of translation competence (Alves & Gonçalves 2007), the role of inferential processes in translation (Alves & Gonçalves 2003; Alves 2007), the role of procedural and declarative knowledge in translation contexts (Alves 2005a), descriptions of cognitive profiles of novice and expert translators (Alves 2005b; Magalhães & Alves 2006), the relevance of domain knowledge as observed in the performance of subject-domain experts who are not translators (Pagano & Silva 2008), the impact of time pressure (Liparini Campos 2005) and translation technology (Alves & Liparini Campos 2009) on the translation process, and also studies on the nature of translation units (see Alves & Vale 2009 for a comprehensive account of this type of research).

2.2 Micro and macro translation units

According to Alves & Vale's (2009) review of the literature on translation units (TU) from the perspective of translation process research, a TU begins with a reading phase that is registered as a pause by Translog key-logging and evolves in a continuous production phase until it is interrupted by a pause. This pause may be a pause for planning or searching for a translation alternative, an assessment of the previous production or the beginning of a new reading phase. As the translation process unfolds, a previously translated segment may be taken up again for revision, deletion or just for consultation without any changes in the text being made. These recurrent movements will be analysed in two ranks, what results in two correlated types of units, namely a micro and a macro TU.

A micro TU is defined as the flow of continuous TT production – which may incorporate the continuous reading of source and TT segments – separated by pauses during the translation process as registered by key-logging and/or eyetracking software. It can be correlated to a ST segment that attracts the trans-lator's focus of attention at a given moment. A macro TU, in turn, is defined as a collection of micro TUs that comprises all the interim text productions that correspond to the translator's focus on the same ST segment from the first tent-ative rendering to the final output that appears in the TT [1]. Thus, a macro TU incorporates all the text production segments (revisions, deletions, substitutions, etc.) in the unfolding of the process, mapped onto the initial focus of attention which triggered a given micro TU. These production segments can be annotated together as a sequence of micro TUs, which then make up a macro TU. Micro and macro TUs consist of text production segments. For the sake of operation-alising the two types of units, micro TUs will consist of a text production seg-ment, including deletions, additions and other possible changes implemented on-line, located between two pauses of arbitrary length, always below the standard threshold of five/six seconds.

Alves & Vale (2009) illustrate the operationalisation of these two concepts. From an initial focus of attention[2] on a given ST segment, several movements may be implemented by the translator at different times of the translation process. Each of these movements constitutes a micro TU until a definite solution is found. The collection of processing steps, from the first draft to the final translation of the text segment is considered to be a macro TU, that is, a macro TU is constituted by micro TUs which are revisions carried out both on-line during the drafting phase and later on at the end-revision phase.[3] As such, revisions carried out while the TT is being drafted can be contrasted and cross-analysed with revisions implemented during a separate phase, after a first version of the TT has been completed.

This two-rank structure of macro TUs comprising one or several micro TUs is proposed to enable the annotation and querying of relevant translation process data. In this chapter, we assume that the analysis of micro and macro TUs, both

---

[1] see Alves & Vale (2009: 261) for a graphic description of a micro/macro TU

[2] A macro TU is a series of translation movements spread throughout the translation process in which the translator writes and edits TT segments that correspond to the same ST segment. This series of movements starts with a focus of attention on the ST segment, the initial focus of attention, and ends with the translator writing the correspondent TT segment that appears as the final product of the translation. The initial focus of attention of a macro TU should not be understood as the translator ocular foci on the screen in the beginning of each micro TU. While there may be one or more ocular foci on both ST and TT in each micro TU, the initial focus of attention of a macro TU is always on the ST and it is what triggers the macro TU.

[3] A micro TU of drafting usually occurs during the drafting phase. Only when the translator misses or deliberately postpones the translation of a segment of the ST, there is a micro TU of drafting during the revision phase. Meanwhile, a micro TU of revision may occur both during the drafting and revision phases of the translation process.

in the drafting and revision phases, can provide direct evidence for describing
different levels of translation performance and identifying segmentation patterns
related to translation expertise [4].

Bearing in mind that the translation unit (TU) and segmentation patterns play
a pivotal role in translation process research, one of the major goals behind the
development of CORPRAT is to investigate the size and the scope of translation
units as defined by Alves (2000). However, until recently, this had to be carried
out manually on relatively small samples. The advent of the LITTERAE search
tool, described in the next section, opens up a new avenue for translation process
research.

2.3 On the development of LITTERAE: mapping micro and macro translation units

LITTERAE[5] is an annotation and search system designed and implemented as a
research tool that is used for storing, annotating and querying corpora of translations comprising both texts and process data. In addition to the corpora, the
system includes a collocation search tool and functions for annotating and querying the corpora.

In designing the annotation system, we have been guided by the following
assumptions that offer challenges, opportunities and restrictions:

1. The system is a web program. It must have a central database and allow
   group work both within premises and by remote access.

2. The system does not impose any specific set of theoretical categories and
   allows the multiple use of different theoretical approaches in the annotation process.

3. The system does not impose any language-specific or theory-specific grammatical structure for its mark-up units. It provides a set abstraction that
   can mark up discontinuous units at any rank of grammatical and process
   hierarchy as well as marking up overlapping units. It does not represent
   composition or constituency and the researcher cannot represent a unit
   may as composed or constitued by others.[6]

---

[4] see also Alves et al. (2010) for an analysis of micro and macro translation units

[5] LITTERAE (http://letra.letras.ufmg.br/litterae) is the direct product of the Laboratory for Experimentation in Translation (LETRA) at Federal University of Minas Gerais (UFMG) in Brazil.

[6] The process annotation is not multi-layer – clauses being composed by groups and phrases –
nor multi-strata – grammatical units representing meaning. It is intended to be a multi-version
annotation in which different versions of the same segment of the text are grouped together.

4. The system keeps raw corpora and annotations separate (stand-off annotation) and thus allows the creation of multiple annotation entries for the same corpus entry. Differently from other systems that replicate raw corpus data in annotation files, annotation entries in LITTERAE replicate no data while a single copy of the raw corpora is kept.[7]

5. The system is designed for both individual and group work. Administrators have control over which parts of the corpora can be accessed by each user, but not over which functions each user may use. If a user has access to a corpus, he or she may do any action the system allows to this corpus.

6. The system is tested against the latest versions of Gecko and Webkit render engines, which are bundled with Firefox, Chrome and Safari web browsers and which can be added as a plugin to the Internet Explorer web browser. These programs/applications are available for the most popular operating systems (Windows, MacOS, Linux, iOS, and Android) free of charge.

Annotating a corpus entry consists of two steps: the first is marking up the corpus entry and the second is tagging its mark-up units with categories. It is possible for a translation process researcher to segment the process by any pause size down to one millisecond, and as the tagging system does not impose any specific set of categories, the researcher can decide which categories to use according to his or her research-specific needs.

The only data abstraction that can be tagged within the annotation system is a TU, operationalised as a set of chunks of a keylog file. By definition, a micro TU ends in a continuous span of writing activity interrupted by a pause of a certain length (Alves 2000). As each writing activity adds a new chunk to the keylog file, by grouping the related writing activities, we are able to mark and tag the macro TU, but this set abstraction may also be used to annotate individual micro TUs and sets of micro TUs related in other ways. The choice of what to annotate is left open to the researchers.

Both the annotation and the corpus entries – texts and process key-logging (generated by Translog 2006 and saved as XML files) – are stored on the same SQL database. They are stored in different relational tables, which results in a completely stand-off annotation. Each corpus entry can be annotated as many times as necessary and the annotations do not interfere with the raw corpus nor

---

[7] LITTERAE stores data in SQL tables, therefore its annotations are entries and not files. Data is not stored in XML files.

with one another. This separation of raw corpora and annotation is achieved by creating multiple distinct isolated mark-ups for each corpus entry (text or process) and by keeping mark-up units in mark-ups instead of inserting the mark-up units into the corpus entries. Each mark-up is identified and stored separately as an isolated entry in a mark-up base apart from the raw corpus base.

The mark-up units are individually tagged with research-specific categories. The tags are also stored in the database separate from the units. When creating charts, tables and querying the corpus, the researchers have the option of choosing a set of annotations to produce a joint output with all related annotations of the research.

Translation process data are stored as raw corpora and are then ready to be annotated. When annotation begins, the researcher will be able to replay the key-log file and interactively select a set of micro units that constitute each macro unit of the translation process. The annotation of mark-up units is implemented in a module of the system code-named Enrich. This is where process data can be enriched on a special replay screen for marking up macro TUs. Log files can be replayed and viewed within different time intervals, the smallest one being one second long. The log file is then segmented by pauses whose value is determined in the box at the top of the screen. Finally, annotations of mark-up units will appear. The system will store annotated process data as macro TUs. Stored information can then be queried using the labels applied in the annotation process.

The final stage of the system allows the querying of larger sets of process data using the labels applied during the annotation process. As shown in §4, researchers will be able to view the annotated macro TUs, search for a specific one, and present the relative and absolute frequency of occurrence of categories as both bar charts and tables. A complete account of the structure and functioning of LITTERAE is found in Alves & Vale (2009).

3 Methodology

3.1 Research design and data collection

The experimental design used in this chapter builds on Alves & Liparini Campos (2009) for data collection and is an extension of Alves & Vale (2009) in terms of categories of analysis. Two correlated source texts, one in English and one in German, consisting of extracts of approximately 500 words, collected from a technical manual, were used as textual input. They contained instructions for the use of a blood sugar meter in English (T1) and in German (T2).

Translations were carried out with access to online documentation sources and no time pressure was introduced. Subjects' performance was recorded with Translog 2000 and data was later converted into XML files with the aid of Translog 2006. Onscreen data not captured by Translog were recorded with the software Camtasia which registered the unfolding of the translation process. Direct observation allowed that notes on translator's behaviour and consultations during the translation task were registered by the researcher in pre-elaborated observation charts.

All procedures followed the methodological approach known as data triangulation (Alves 2003), which attempts to map the translation process using data collected from different vantage points [8]. Sources for triangulating translation process data were the recordings of target text production in real time, direct observation charts registering notes on translator's consultation and behaviour, and retrospective protocols. For the purpose of the present chapter, only Translog XML files were analysed with the aid of the LITTERAE search tool.

3.2 Methodology for data analysis

Data generated in the experiment consisted of 12 target texts in Brazilian Portuguese. Pauses which occurred during their production were classified as micro units on the basis of a five second pause interval. Each of these micro units received a time stamp. Whenever these micro units remain unchanged throughout the translation process, they are considered to be a macro unit. And whenever one of these micro units is taken up again by the translators, they are grouped together and, as such, also considered to be a macro unit. In this chapter, we only analysed macro units of the latter kind using the annotation procedures provided by LITTERAE. As a methodological decision, micro units were classified as instances of online revision when the subsequent micro unit was processed again still in the drafting phase. These were grouped together and identified as a macro unit by their corresponding time stamps and their editing was represented by a pipe [|]. When the micro unit was taken up again in the end-revision phase, it was identified with a corresponding time stamp which was far apart in terms of temporal dislocation from the preceding micro unit in the drafting phase. This type of editing in the revision phase was represented by a tilde [~].

(1)   *ned | medidor de açúcar | medidor do nível de açúcar* – [P1]

(2)   *fora do corpo ~ de forma invasiva* – [P2]

---

[8] see also Jakobsen (1999) for a discussion of this technique originally used in the social sciences

(3)   *Medidor de índice | Medidor de glicemis ~ Medidor de glicemia* – [P3]

Example 1 presents two revision steps and three versions of a text segment. It was captured during the drafting phase in four chunks of the translog file. Together they make up a macro unit. Editing within a macro unit is represented by a pipe [|]. As shown in Figure 1, there are four chunks of writing activity in this macro unit: at 62730ms of the translation process the translator typed *(ned*; after approximately two seconds, at 88830ms, the three first letters were deleted and *medidor de* 'meter of' was typed in; around two seconds later, at 106300ms, after a pause for internal support, *açúcar no sangue)* 'sugar in the blood' was typed; then, at 1228840ms, still in the drafting phase, *do nível* 'of the level' was inserted. This generated the end product *medidor do nível de açúcar no sangue* 'meter of the level of sugar in the blood' or 'blood sugar level meter' which appears in the TT.[9] This type of macro unit was classified as P1, namely a macro unit with processing patterns which occur only in the drafting phase.

Apply tag	Tag Name	P1 ×		Delete
ned	medidor de açúcar	medidor do nível açúcar	62730: (ned * ⊗		
		88830: ⊗ ⊗ ⊗medidor de		
		106300: açúcar no sangue)		
		1228840: [Mouse][Mouse]nível [Mouse][Mouse]⊗0[Mouse][Mouse]		

Figure 1: Example of a macro translation unit type P1

In Example 2, two micro units were processed in different phases of the translation process to make up a macro translation unit. As shown in Figure 2, first a micro unit was observed in the drafting phase at 792480ms in a long text segment of 115 characters in which the expression *fora do corpo* 'outside the body' appeared. This provisional solution was only revised in the revision phase. After a first draft of the target text had been produced, at 3596240ms the micro unit was changed into *de forma invasiva* 'in an invasive manner' which together with the first rendering makes up a macro unit. Editing within a macro unit which occurs in the revision phase is represented by a tilde [~]. This type of macro unit was classified as P2, namely a macro unit with processing patterns which occur only once in the drafting phase and are then taken up again during the revision phase.

In Example 3, two micro units occur in the drafting phase as in a P1 type of macro translation unit. However, differently from a P1 macro unit, there is also

---

[9] The segment of the text that is targeted by micro TUs of edition is generally smaller than the entire segment of text produced in micro TUs of revision. When representing the revision chain and the iterim versions, we only present the smaller segments that are actually reviewed.

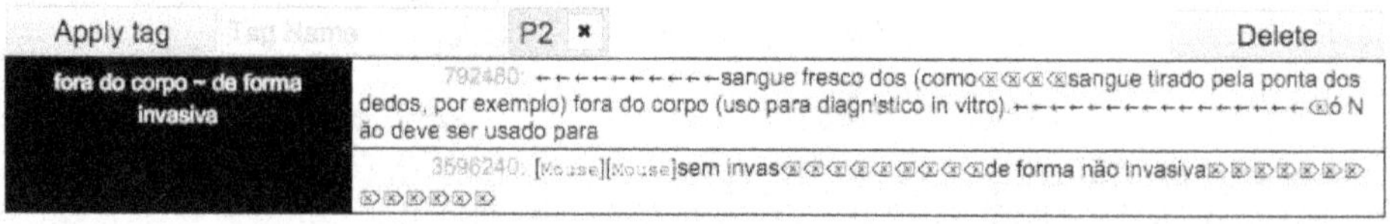

Figure 2: Example of a macro translation unit type P2

one (or more) micro unit observed in the revision phase. As shown in Figure 3, at 58130ms the micro unit was processed as *medidor de índice* 'meter of index'. Next, still in the drafting phase, it was changed into *medidor de glicemis* 'meter of blood-sugar-leves /typo/'. Then, at 2108600, during the revision phase, the typo "s" was deleted and replaced by "a" to render *medidor de glicemia* 'meter of blood-sugar-level'. This type of macro unit was classified as P3, namely a macro unit with processing patterns which occur more than once in the drafting phase and are taken up again once or more in the revision phase.

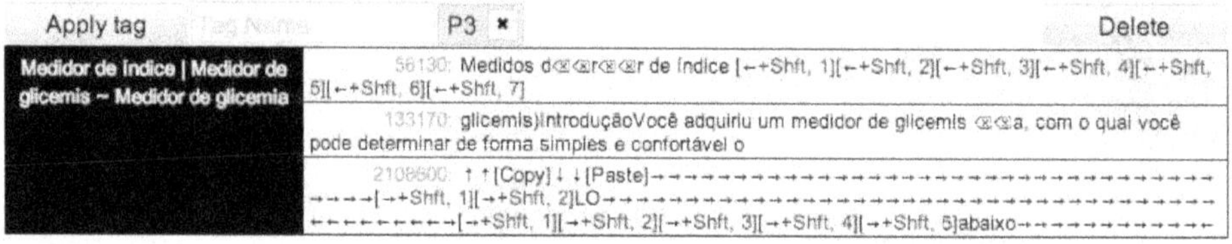

Figure 3: Example of a macro translation unit type P3

In order to carry out the analysis of drafting and revision patterns, XML files with translation process data from the 12 professional translators were segmented into micro units. Each file was then annotaded manually on the basis of the triadic classification, and micro units were classified as P1, P2 and P3. The same procedure was applied to all 12 XML files with translation process data generated by Translog 2006. [10] Using these three categories, all micro units registered in the 12 keylog files with translation process data were annotated as macro units. The next section presents the results of this classification.

---

[10] For the sake of clarification, we provide a link http://letra.letras.ufmg.br/resources/2010_alves_vale.png (last accessed 2011-11-24) with access to three appendixes where data analysis is fully displayed. Appendix 1 contains a set of annotated macro units of type P1 whereas Appendix 2 comprises all macro units classified as P2 and Appendix 3 shows the remaining macro units classified as P3.

4 Data analysis

In accordance with the proposal made by Alves & Vale (2009) to classify micro and macro translation units, our corpus contains 355 macro units implemented by the 12 subjects. Table 1 shows the total number of macro units, made up by a combination of P1, P2 and P3 types.

Table 1: Total number of macro units per subject

Subject E1	Number of macro units (P1 + P2 + P3) =	
E1	(17 + 21 + 1) =	39
E2	(7 + 0 + 0) =	07
E3	(9 + 12 + 0) =	21
E4	(29 + 22 + 5) =	56
E5	(4 + 58 + 1) =	63
E6	(11 + 10 + 0) =	21
G1	(12 + 29 + 5) =	46
G2	(6 + 5 + 2) =	13
G3	(23 + 0 + 0) =	23
G4	(22 + 12 + 2) =	36
G5	(1 + 8 + 0) =	09
G6	(10 + 10 + 1) =	21
Total	(151 + 187 + 17) =	355

By looking at Table 1, one can easily identify a completely different pattern in E5 with 58 occurrences of type P2 and only 4 cases of P1 and 1 case of P3. The next highest count in this category is observed in the performance of G1 with 29 occurences of P2. If we consider E5 as an outlier, the total number of P1 will be 147, with 129 cases of P2 and 16 occurrences of P3, indicating that, on the whole, P1 > P2 > P3. As we have different profiles and different revision total frequencies, the total numbers of P1, P2, and P3 are not informative in themselves. Comparing total P1 and total P2 will result in different rules depending on the profiles we exclude. However, regardless of considering E5 as an outlier or not, P1 and P2 occurrences are far higher than P3 types which makes only 4.8% of the total number of occurrences in the sample.

4.1 Identifying patterns of translation units and profiles during drafting and revision

Table 2 presents the absolute and relative numbers across the sample, separating data among the subjects who translated from English (E1-E6) and from German into Brazilian Portuguese (G1-G6), grouping them according to P1, P2 and P3 types of macro translation units and adding a column with a classification of translator profiles which will be discussed further in this section.

Table 2: Absolute and relative numbers for P1, P2 and P3 per subject and corresponding profiles

Subject	P1		P2		P3		Profile	Sub-profile
	Abs.	Rel.	Abs.	Rel.	Abs.	Rel.		
E1	17	43.7%	21	53.8%	1	2.6%	Drafter/Reviser	Non-Recursive
E2	7	100%	0	----	0	----	Drafter	
E3	9	42.9%	12	57.1%	0	----	Drafter/Reviser	Non-Recursive
E4	29	51.8%	22	39.2%	5	8.9%	Drafter/Reviser	Recursive
E5	4	6.3%	58	92.0%	1	1.6%	Reviser	
E6	11	52.4%	10	47.6%	0	----	Drafter/Reviser	Non-Recursive
G1	12	26.1%	29	63.0%	5	10.9%	Drafter/Reviser	Recursive
G2	6	46.2%	5	38.5%	2	15.4%	Drafter/Reviser	Recursive
G3	23	100%	0	----	0	----	Drafter	
G4	22	61.1%	12	33.3%	2	5.6%	Drafter/Reviser	Recursive
G5	1	11.1%	8	88.9%	0	----	Reviser	
G6	10	47.6%	10	47.6%	1	4.8%	Drafter/Reviser	Non-Recursive

If we look at the apparently disparate figures displayed in Table 2, a picture of idiosyncratic patterns might seem to be the first obvious conclusion. However, by closer scrutiny we can identify correlated patterns across the two language pairs. On the one hand, both E2 and G3 only show cases of P1 macro units whereas E5 and G5 display predominant occurrences of P2 macro units. On the other hand, the remaining subjects show a pattern where P1 and P2 types of macro units compete in terms of predominance and sometimes P1 > P2 and at other times P2 > P1. If we apply a formula to the number of occurrences, we can classify the data into four different translator profiles.

A translator was classified with the profile of a "Drafter" if, during the drafting phase, he or she revised the TT six times more than during the revision phase. Inversely, a translator was classified with the profile of a "Reviser" if, during the revision phase, he or she revised the TT six times more than during the drafting phase. The remaining translators were classified with the profile of a "Drafter/Reviser". Within this group, we found two special subgroups comprised by translators who either revised the same parts of the TT both during the drafting and the revision phases, revisions of the type P3 (Recursive sub-profile) and those who did not (Non-recursive sub-profile). Table 3 displays the formulae for calculating the four different profiles.

Table 3: Calculation of translator profiles per types of macro TUs where < or > 1/6 is a distinctive indicator

Drafter	$(P2 + P3) \div P1 < 1/6$
Reviser	$P1 \div (P2 + P3) < 1/6$
Drafter Non-Recursive Revise	$(P2 + P3) \div P1 \geq 1/6$ & $P2 \div P3 < 1/6$
Drafter Recursive Reviser	$(P2 + P3) \div P1 \geq 1/6$ & $P2 \div P3 \geq 1/6$

4.2 Patterns of translator profiles in the drafting and in the revision phases

According to our analysis, we identified four types of profiles: Drafters, Revisers, Drafter Non-Recursive Revisers, and Drafter Recursive Revisers. Drafters are those subjects who predominantly show P1 types of macro translation units and process them entirely during the drafting phase. Revisers, on the other hand, seem to produce interim solutions in the provisional target text while drafting and implementing changes predominantly in the revision phase. As far as the third and fourth profiles are concerned, those of the Drafter/Reviser, all subjects had approximately the same number of TT changes in both phases, which can be expressed by $1/2 < P1 \div (P2 + P3) < 2$.

The data analysis shows that neither $1/6 < (P2 + P3) \div P1 < 1/2$ nor $1/6 < P1 \div (P2 + P3) < 1/2$ were observed in the sample. In other words, either the subject had an approximate equal number of changes during the drafting and revision phases or the subject implemented a lot more changes in one phase than in the other. In our corpus, there is no subject with a tendency to revise slightly more in one of the two phases. There are two trends in the sample: a predominant mode of revision either during the drafting or revision phases or a strong tendency towards a balanced distribution of P1 and P2 types of macro translation units.

When determining the "Drafter Recursive Reviser" profile, all translators of the Drafter Reviser profile were found to have approximately six times more changes implemented of type P2 than those of type P3. The ones that are over the threshold of 6 P2s per P3 are on the "Drafter Non-Recursive Reviser" profile and the ones who were below this threshold were on the "Drafter Recursive Reviser" profile. Again, all translators were close to this threshold. Therefore, these two categories can be understood as slight tendencies in a cline.

At last, by definition, there must be at least one change during the drafting phase for identifying a textual change of the type P3, which can be expressed as P1 > 0 if P3 > 0. Although this is the only rule that must be found by definition, we also found two other rules: in every analysed translation, there were more changes in the drafting phase (P1) than recursive changes in the revision phase (P3) and there were always more non-recursive changes in the revision phase (P2) than recursive ones (P3), what can be expressed as P1 > P3 and P2 > P3.

4.3 Patterns of macro translation units in the drafting and in the revision phases

Besides classifying the data in terms of macro translation units of types P1, P2 and P3 as well as introducing four different translator profiles, the data analysis also allows the observation of subpatterns within the triadic categories. By looking at the data, one observes how decisions previously made by the translator influence the revision patterns in the unfolding of the macro translation units. On the one hand, translation process data such as key-logging is linear in time – one event at a time follows another – and recursive in the TT: additions, editions and deletions may happen in any position of it. On the other hand, TTs have a linear structure: their characters – in all their intermediate and final versions – are organized linearly – one character after the other. When translating a given micro unit, a choice made at timestamp X may lead the translator to replace a decision made in a previous part of the TT at timestamp Y by an alternative which signals an attempt to standardize choices. This upward movement has been classified as a P1 ascending pattern as shown in Figure 4.

As displayed in the upper part of Figure 4, one can see that, as shown at timestamp 471290ms, G4 initially translates the German verb *bestimmen* 'determine' into Brazilian Portuguese as *determinar* 'determine'. As the process unfolds, two lexical items are translated as *medição* and *medida* 'measurement'. Then, as shown at timestamp 557820ms, still in the drafting phase, after translating the noun *Bestimmung* 'determination' as *medição* 'measurement', G4 changes *determinar* 'determine' into *mensurar* 'measure'. This upward recursive movement in text production seems to be clearly driven by the lexical choices of *medição/medida* 'measurement' and *medição* 'measurement' which lead G4 to replace *determinar* by *mensurar*. The upward unfolding of the micro units into a macro unit in the drafting phase illustrates what we call a P1 ascending pattern.

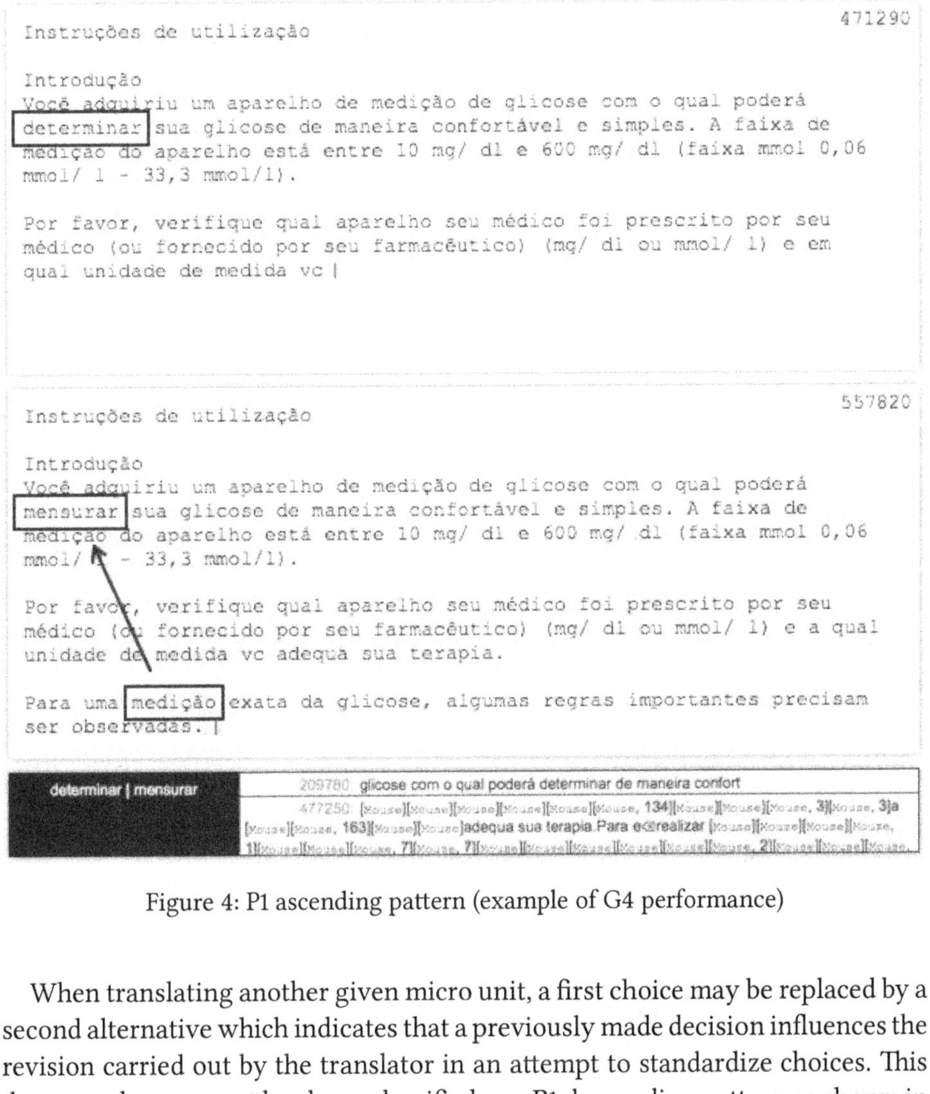

Figure 4: P1 ascending pattern (example of G4 performance)

When translating another given micro unit, a first choice may be replaced by a second alternative which indicates that a previously made decision influences the revision carried out by the translator in an attempt to standardize choices. This downward movement has been classified as a P1 descending pattern as shown in Figure 5.

As displayed in the upper part of Figure 5, one can see that, at timestamp 690820ms, while translating the same source text fragment, G6 initially translates the German verb *bestimmen* 'determine' into Brazilian Portuguese as *verificar* 'verify'. Figure 5 also shows that *Bestimmungen* 'determinations' down below in the same source text fragment was translated as *averiguações* 'investigations'. As the process unfolds, at timestamp 738950ms, still in the drafting phase, G6

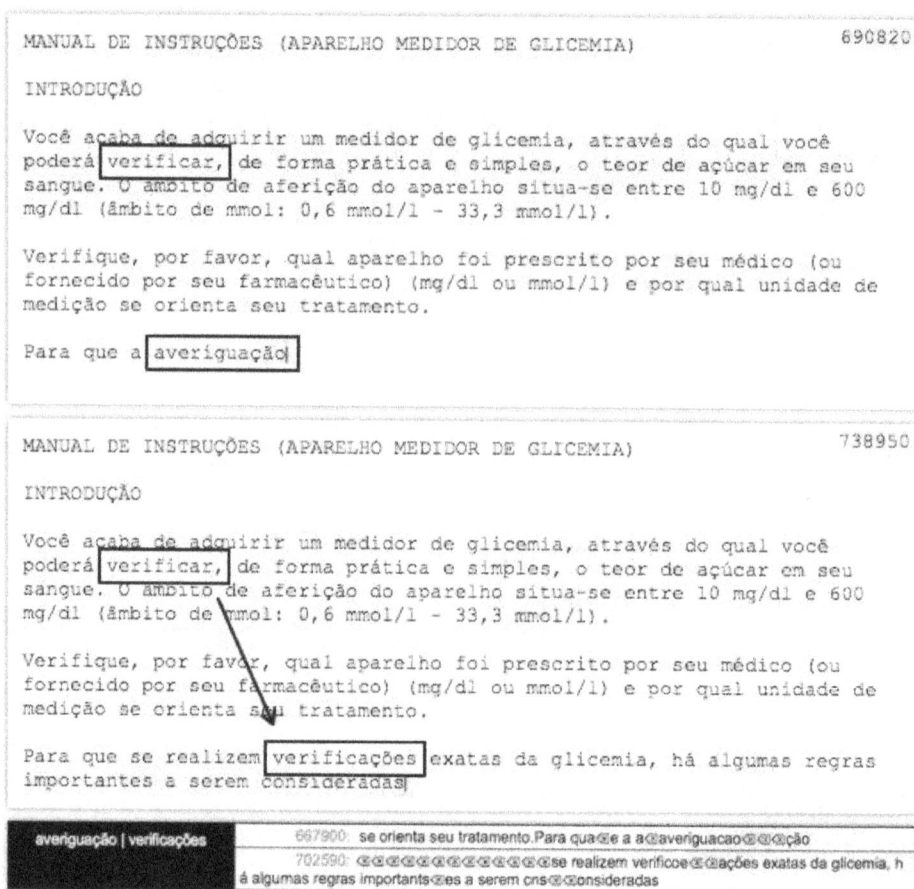

Figure 5: P1 descending pattern (example of G6 performance)

changes *averiguações* 'investigations' into *verificações* 'verifications'. This downward recursive movement in text production seems to be clearly driven by the lexical choice of *verificar* 'verify' at shown timestamp 690820ms. The downward unfolding of the micro units into a macro unit in the drafting phase illustrates what we call a P1 descending pattern.

Both ascending and descending subtypes of P1 signal the influence of different stages of text production in the unfolding of macro translation units. What must be clear is that the notion of descending and ascending movements is related to but is not the same as the one of previous and following positions in the TT. The former are dynamic movements of the subjects over the TT in a process-oriented perspective and the latter are static relative positions of text segments in a product-oriented perspective. Sometimes the driving force is a translation de-cision made later in the drafting phase which influences the revision of a choice which had already been made earlier in the translation process (P1 ascending pat-tern). At other times, the driving force is a previously made decision which seems to guide the revision of a translation alternative which is then implemented on the basis of a choice made at a previous timestamp (P1 descending pattern).

Additionally, similar processes of descending types of macro units seem to occur when we move away from the drafting phase. Given our observations of P-types, P2 only shows a descending pattern. In this subtype of macro translation unit, a micro unit occurs only once in the drafting phase and is then processed once or more in the revision phase.

Figure 6 displays an example of a P2 descending pattern. As displayed in the upper part of Figure 6, one can see that E3 initially translates the pair 'adjust' and 'set up' by *regular* 'regulate' and *definiu* 'defined'. E3 then changes *definiu* 'defined' into *regulou* 'regulated' during the revision phase. The downward un-folding of the micro units into a macro unit in the revision phase illustrates what we call a P2 descending pattern.

Finally, as shown in Figure 7, a descending pattern also seems to be prototyp-ical of P3.

One can see that G6 translates the word set *bestimmen, Messbereich, Bereich, kontrollieren, Bestimmungen* by *verificar* 'verify', *âmbito de aferição* 'scope of veri-fication', *âmbito de aferição* 'scope of verification', *verifique* 'verify', *verificações* 'verifications' and then changes *verificações* 'verifications' into *aferições* 'verific-ations' in the revision phase. These examples of changes in the revision phase show a revision process that is not bound to the lexical correspondences between the source and target languages/texts.

5 Concluding remarks

The picture emerging from the data analysis is manifold. Using the LITTERAE annotation and search tool, it was possible to classify macro translation units according to types P1, P2 and P3. It was also possible to differentiate two main types of macro translation units. On the one hand, P1 can be considered as a type of macro unit which signals online cognitive processing of translation units both in ascending and descending modes. On the other hand, P2 and P3 can be seen as types of macro units which signal a somewhat different process, namely a process that is more detached from the source text and consists of revisions of text production rather than translations per se. This difference is quite striking

```
A verificação do nível de açúcar no sangue pode ser a grande diferença
para você saber como gerenciar seu diabete diariamente. Foi elaborado
da forma mais simples e confortável possível. Os medidores AC são
fáceis de usar e você pode regular o Dispositivo de lancetamento para
executar o teste mais confortavelmente.

INFORMAÇÕES IMPORTANTES
. Seu medidor de glicose foi projetado e aprovado para tirar
amostragens de sangue fresco dos capilares (sangue tirado pela ponta
dos dedos, por exemplo) de forma não invasiva (uso para diagnóstico in
vitro). Não deve ser usado para diagnosticar a presença de diabetes.

EXECUÇÃO DE UM TESTE DE SANGUE

Antes de executar seu primeiro teste, verifique se você definiu
corretamente o medidor e faça um teste de controle.
```

```
A verificação do nível de açúcar no sangue pode ser a grande diferença
para você saber como gerenciar seu diabete diariamente. Foi elaborado
da forma mais simples e confortável possível. Os medidores AC são
fáceis de usar e você pode regular o Dispositivo de lancetamento para
executar o teste mais confortavelmente.

INFORMAÇÕES IMPORTANTES
. Seu medidor de glicose foi projetado e aprovado para tirar
amostragens de sangue fresco dos capilares (sangue tirado pela ponta
dos dedos, por exemplo) de forma não invasiva (uso para diagnóstico in
vitro). Não deve ser usado para diagnosticar a presença de diabetes.

EXECUÇÃO DE UM TESTE DE SANGUE

Antes de executar seu primeiro teste, verifique se você regulou
corretamente o medidor e faça um teste de controle.
```

| definiu – regulou | 962390: você concⒼ-Ⓔ-Ⓔdefiniu ciⒺorretamente o medidor e faça um teste de controle.1. La ve e seque suas mãos.2. |
| | 3624080: ↓↓↓↓↓↓↓↓↓↓↓↓↓↓↓[Mouse][Mouse][Mouse, 8][Mouse, 8]regulou [Mouse][Mouse]↓ ↓↓↓↓↓↓↓↓↓↓↓↓↓↓[Mouse][Mouse]←Ⓒin[Mouse][Mouse][Mouse][Mouse] |

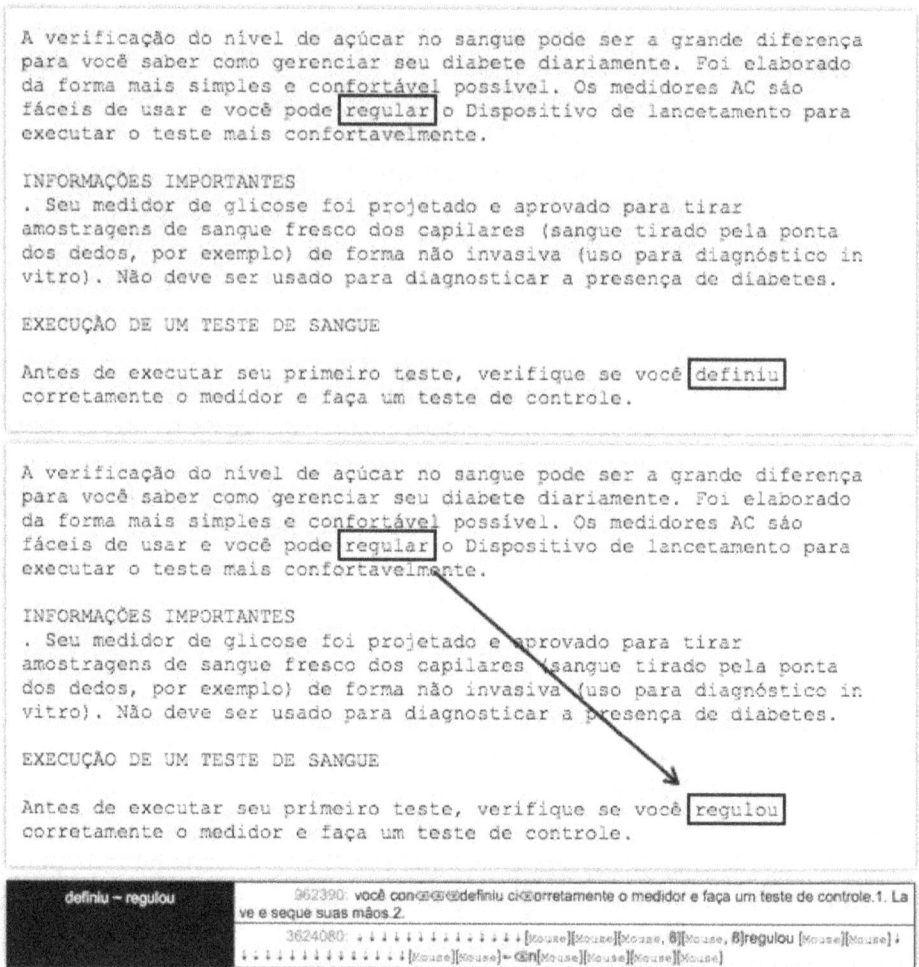

Figure 6: P2 descending pattern (example of E3 performance)

particularly in view of the fact that both P2 and P3 are descending modes of text production in translation. On the whole, P2 types are more frequent than P3 types and more substantial revisions are only found among P2 types of macro translation units. P3 types seem to account for more fine-grained revisions which are quite small in numbers.

The overall trend shows that in terms of cognitive processing P1 has quite a distinctive nature than that of P2 and P3 and seems to be where translation takes place par excellence. However, the amount of data analysed in this chapter is too small to allow for generalizations. Nevertheless, we hope to have paved the

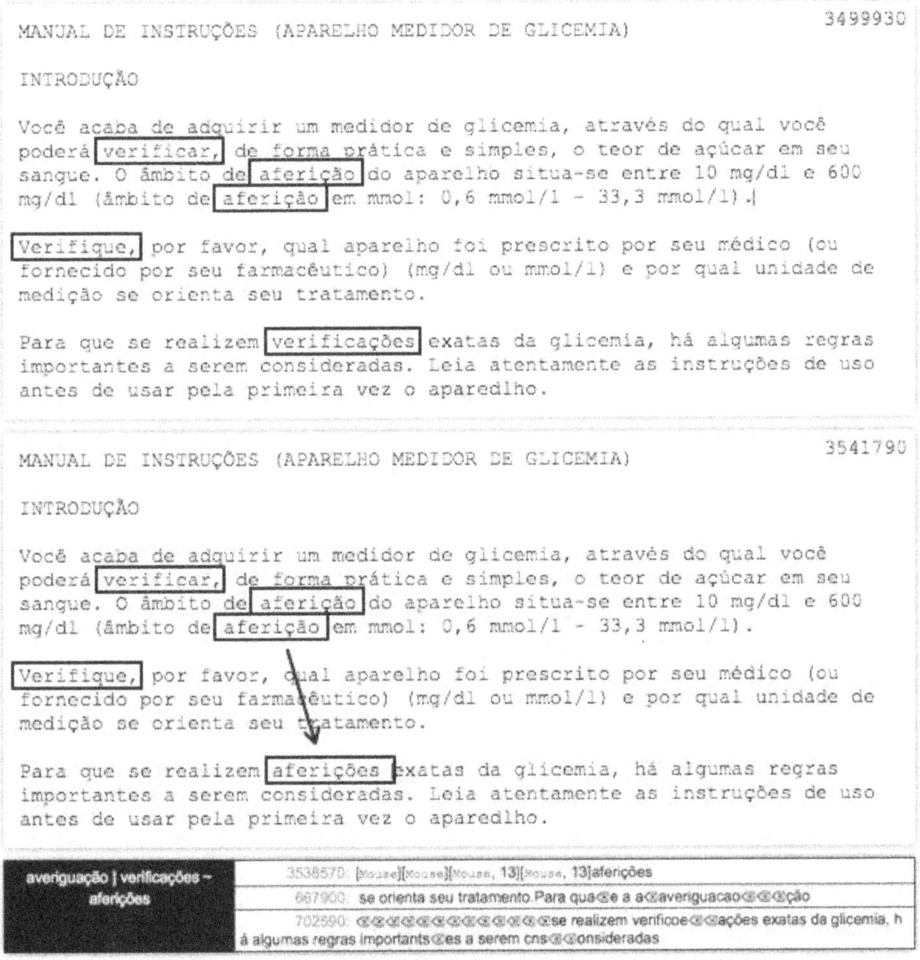

Figure 7: P3 descending pattern (example of G6 performance)

way for future studies by presenting a tool and a methodology which can be replicated and, thus, foster a corpus linguistics oriented analysis of translation process data.

Acknowledgements

Research developed within the framework of the SEGTRAD Project (Cognitive Segmentation and Translation Memory Systems: investigating the interface between translators' performance and translation technology) was funded by the Brazilian Research Council (CNPq) grant n° 301270/2005-8.

References

Alves, Fabio. 2000. Unidades de tradução: O que são e como operá-las. In Fábio Alves, Célia Magalhães & Adriana S. Pagano (eds.), *Traduzir com autonomia: Estratégias para o tradutor em formação*, 29–38. São Paulo: Contexto.

Alves, Fabio (ed.). 2003. *Triangulating translation: Perspectives in process-oriented research*. Amsterdam: John Benjamins.

Alves, Fabio. 2005a. Bridging the gap between declarative and procedural knowledge in the training of translators: Meta-reflection under scrutiny. *Meta. Revue des Traductéurs* 50(4).

Alves, Fabio. 2005b. Ritmo cognitivo, meta-função e experiência: Parâmetros de análise processual no desempenho de tradutores novatos e experientes. In Fabio Alves, Magalhães Célia & Adriana S. Pagano (eds.), *Competência em tradução: Cognição e discurso*, 109–169. Belo Horizonte: Editora UFMG.

Alves, Fabio. 2007. Cognitive effort and contextual effect in translation: A relevance-theoretic approach. *Journal of Translation Studies* 1(10). 18–35.

Alves, Fabio & José Luiz Gonçalves. 2003. A relevance theory approach to the investigation of inferential processes in translation. In Alves Favio (ed.), *Triangulating translation: Perspectives in process oriented research*, 3–24. Amsterdam: John Benjamins.

Alves, Fabio & José Luiz Gonçalves. 2007. Modelling translator's competence: Relevance and expertise under scrutiny. In Yves Gambier, Miriam Shlesinger & Radegundis Stolze (eds.), *Translation studies: Doubts and directions. Selected papers from the IV congress of the European Society for Translation Studies*, 41–55. Amsterdam: John Benjamins.

Alves, Fabio & Tânia Liparini Campos. 2009. Translation technology in time: Investigating the impact of translation memory systems and time pressure on types of internal and external support. In Susanne Göpferich, Arnt L. Jakobsen & Inger Mees (eds.), *Behind the mind: methods, models and results in translation process research*. 191–218. Copenhagen: Samfundslitteratur.

Alves, Fabio & Daniel Couto Vale. 2009. Probing the unit of translation in time: Aspects of the design and development of a web application for storing, annotating, and querying translation process data. *Across Languages and Cultures* 2(10). 251–273.

Alves, Fabio, Adriana S. Pagano, Stella Neumann, Erich Steiner & Silvia Hansen-Schirra. 2010. Translation units and grammatical shifts: Towards an integration of product- and process-based translation research. In Gregory M. Shreve & Erik Angelone (eds.), *Translation and cognition*, 109–142. Amsterdam: John Benjamins.

Ghadessy, Mohsen & Yanjie Gao. 2001. Small corpora and translation: Comparing thematic organization in two languages. In Ghadessy Mohsen, Alex Henry & Robert L. Roseberry (eds.), *Small corpus studies and ELT: Theory and practice*. 335–362. Amsterdam: John Benjamins.

Hansen-Schirra, Silvia, Stella Neumann & Erich Steiner. 2007. Cohesive explicitness and explicitation in an English-German translation corpus. *Languages in Contrast* 2(7). 241–265.

Jakobsen, Arnt L. 1999. Logging target text production with Translog. In Gyde Hansen (ed.), *Probing the process in translation: Methods and results*, 9–20. Copenhagen: Samfundslitteratur.

Jakobsen, Arnt L. 2002. Translation, drafting and revision by professional translators and by translation students. In Gyde Hansen (ed.), *Empirical translation studies: Process and product*, 191–204. Copenhagen: Samfundslitteratur.

Liparini Campos, Tânia. 2005. *O efeito da pressão de tempo na realização de tarefas de tradução: Uma análise processual sobre o desempenho de tradutores em formação*. Unpublished MA Thesis, Federal University of Minas Gerais, Brazil.

Magalhães, Célia Maria & Fabio Alves. 2006. Investigando o papel do monitoramento cognitivo-discursivo e da meta-reflexão na formação de tradutores. *Cadernos de Tradução* 1(17). 71–128.

Olohan, Maeve & Mona Baker. 2000. Reporting 'that' in translated English: Evidence for subconscious processes of explicitation? *Across Languages and Cultures* 2(1). 141–158.

Pagano, Adriana S., Célia Maria Magalhães & Fabio Alves. 2004. Towards the construction of a multilingual, multifunctional corpus: Factors in the design and applications of CORDIALL. *Tradterm* 1(10). 143–151.

Pagano, Adriana S. & Igor A. L. Silva. 2008. Domain knowledge in translation task execution: Insights from academic researchers performing as translators. In *Proceedings of the XVIII FIT world congress*. CD-ROM. Shanghai: Foreign Language Press.

Chapter 6

Computerlinguistik in der Dolmetschpraxis unter besonderer Berücksichtigung der Korpusanalyse

Claudio Fantinuoli

Johannes Gutenberg-Universität Mainz in Germersheim

Erfolgreiches Dolmetschen setzt qualifizierte Vorbereitung voraus. Dazu gehören die nutzeradäquate Gestaltung und die kontinuierliche Pflege von Terminologiebeständen sowie die Möglichkeit auf mehrsprachige Informationen und Terminologie schnell und effizient zugreifen zu können. Um die Vorbereitungsphase zu optimieren und zu rationalisieren wird ein dolmetschorientierter Korpus-Ansatz beschrieben und eine dafür entwickelte Terminologie- und Wissensmanagementsoftware vorgestellt. Für die Konferenzvorbereitung implementiert die Software Funktionalitäten wie automatische Termextraktion, automatische Herstellung von Fachkorpora und die Möglichkeit der Informationssuche aus strukturierten Webressourcen. Darüber hinaus bietet das Tool Module zur Verwaltung der gewonnenen Informationen und zum dolmetschfreundlichen Abrufen der in Glossaren fixierten Terminologiebestände. In diesem Artikel sollen die relevanten Grundlagen der Dolmetschwissenschaft und einige Module der implementierten Software vorgestellt werden.

1 Der Dolmetscher und der Dolmetscherberuf

Dolmetscher arbeiten per definitionem in einem multilingualen Umfeld. Sie übertragen einen mündlich dargebotenen Text von einer Ausgangsprache in eine Zielsprache und dienen dem unmittelbaren Verständnis der am Kommunikationsprozess beteiligten Teilnehmer.

Grundsätzlich wird zwischen drei Formen des Dolmetschens unterschieden: dem Gesprächsdolmetschen, dem Konsekutivdolmetschen und dem Simultandolmetschen. Beim Gesprächsdolmetschen – je nach Einsatzbereich, Setting und

Claudio Fantinuoli. 2017. Computerlinguistik in der Dolmetschpraxis unter besonderer Berücksichtigung der Korpusanalyse. In Silvia Hansen-Schirra, Stella Neumann & Oliver Čulo (Hrsg.), *Annotation, exploitation and evaluation of parallel corpora*, 111–146. Berlin: Language Science Press. DOI:10.5281/zenodo.283501

Land auch „Gerichtsdolmetschen", „Verhandlungsdolmetschen", „Community Interpreting", „Kommunaldolmetschen" oder „Fachdolmetschen" genannt – findet die Übertragung eines Textes bidirektional zwischen mindestens zwei Kommunikationspartnern statt, die in einer dialogischen Interaktion sukzessiv von Textproduzenten zu Textrezipienten werden. Beim Konsekutivdolmetschen findet die Übertragung eines Textes dagegen in einer meist nicht dialogischen Interaktion monodirektional von einer Sprache in die andere statt. Dies geschieht zeitversetzt, und zwar nachdem der Textproduzent den gesamten Text oder einen Teil davon zu Ende vorgetragen hat. Auch beim Simultandolmetschen wird der Text monodirektional in die Zielsprache übertragen, jedoch (fast) gleichzeitig zu seiner Äußerung.[1] Um die Simultanität der Übertragung zu ermöglichen, bedienen sich Dolmetscher technischer Einrichtungen, d.h. schalldichten Kabinen, Kopfhörern und Mikrophonen. Aufgrund des typischen Settings – Kongresse, Tagungen, Seminare, usw. –, in dem sie Anwendung finden, werden das Konsekutiv- und Simultandolmetschen traditionell auch als Konferenzdolmetschen bezeichnet.

Die hier aufgeführte Unterscheidung und Bezeichnung der Hauptdolmetschformen sind keineswegs als exhaustiv oder definitiv zu betrachten. Vielmehr bewegt sich jede Form des Dolmetschens in einem begrifflichen Kontinuum zwischen Konferenzdolmetschen (KD) und Nicht-Konferenzdolmetschen (NKD).[2] In diesem Beitrag wird insbesondere auf das Konferenzdolmetschen eingegangen. Ein besonderes Augenmerk gilt dabei dem Simultandolmetschen, der gegenwärtig am häufigsten eingesetzten Form des Konferenzdolmetschens.

Die Heterogenität und Spezifität der Konferenzthemen verlangt von den Dolmetschern, in der Regel keine Experten des auf der Konferenz behandelten Faches, die Bereitschaft und Fähigkeit, sich ständig in neue Fachgebiete einzuarbeiten (vgl. Kalina 2007; Andres 2011). Für die Vorbereitung steht den Dolmetschern meist sehr wenig Zeit zur Verfügung, da innerhalb eines relativ kurzen Zeitraumes mehrere thematisch unterschiedliche Einsätze bewältigt werden müssen. So gehört es beispielsweise zum Alltag der Dolmetscher, dass sie sich innerhalb nur weniger Tage auf eine Bilanzpressekonferenz, eine technische Schulung und ein medizinisches Symposium vorbereiten müssen. Sehr oft findet das erworbene Wissen nur für einen einzelnen Einsatz Verwendung. Auf internationalen Fachkonferenzen wird die Kommunikation unter den Experten, die zwar ein entsprechendes Fachwissen, jedoch keine gemeinsame Sprache miteinander teilen,

---

[1] Die Zeitversetzung zwischen Äußerung und Verdolmetschung wird in der Dolmetschwissenschaft „Decalage" genannt und beträgt einige Sekunden (vgl. Pöchhacker 2004).

[2] Zur weiteren Differenzierung und Annäherung zwischen den vielen Typologien von Dolmetschformen vgl. Feldweg (1996: 25ff), Kalina (2001: 51), Pöchhacker (2000: 33) und Gross-Dinter (2009: 354ff)

durch zumeist fachfremde Personen – die Dolmetscher – ermöglicht. Aus der Perspektive der stattfindenden Kommunikation entsteht dabei eine Laien-Experten-Konstellation (vgl. Will 2009). Generell manifestiert sich das daraus resultierende Ungleichgewicht auf drei Ebenen:

- Inhalt

- Terminologie

- Phraseologie

Die inhaltliche Ebene betrifft das Fachwissen. Die Kommunikation unter den Konferenzteilnehmern basiert auf einem hohen Grad an Vorwissen, das in unterschiedlichem Maße von den Textproduzenten und Textrezipienten geteilt wird. Ohne dieses Wissen kann die Kommunikation nicht stattfinden, da Schlüsselkompetenzen fehlen, die erforderlich sind, um Sachverhalte richtig zu verstehen. Die terminologische Ebene betrifft die Fachterminologie, d.h. die Gesamtheit aller Fachtermini, die einem oder mehreren Gebieten zugeordnet werden können und die auf einer Konferenz verwendet werden, um fachliche Informationen auszutauschen. Nur mit der richtigen Terminologie kann eine reibungslose Fachkommunikation stattfinden, da diese in allen Fachbereichen die Grundlage der schriftlichen und mündlichen Fachkommunikation bildet (vgl. Arntz, Picht & Mayer 2009: 6). Die phraseologische Ebene betrifft die fachgebundene Ausdrucksweise, die durch die sogenannten „Fachwendungen" (Picht 1990: 207) ihren Ausdruck findet. Unter Fachwendungen versteht man die Verbindung von mindestens zwei sprachlichen Elementen zur Äußerung eines fachlichen Inhaltes. Rossenbeck beschreibt diese Fachwendungen – auch Fachphraseologie genannt – als „die Gesamtheit der Wortbildungen, deren Bestandteile sich zu einer charakteristischen Kombination verfestigt haben und die in Texten eines bestimmten Fachgebiets zu beobachten sind" (Rossenbeck 1989: 199). Bei der phraseologischen Ebene geht es um die Wahl bestimmter Ausdrücke, Phrasen, Kollokationen, etc., die typischerweise von den Konferenzteilnehmern verwendet werden. Da sich auf derartigen Veranstaltungen Insider eines Fachgebietes einfinden, verwenden diese einen bestimmten „in-house jargon" (Kalina 2005: 777), eine eigene gemeinsame Fachsprache. Beispiele hierfür sind spezifische Verbalverbindungen des Typs *Abtragspartikeln ausschwemmen*, *ein Testament errichten* und *eine Aktie zeichnen*.

Um der fachlichen Kommunikationssituation gerecht werden zu können, müssen Dolmetscher folglich alle drei Ebenen gut beherrschen. Sie müssen über genügend fachliches Vorwissen verfügen, um die Zusammenhänge (schnell) erfassen und Informationen von einer Sprache in eine andere übertragen zu können. Sie müssen die verwendete Terminologie in den zu verdolmetschenden Sprachen kennen und parat haben, um den reibungslosen und eindeutigen mehrsprachigen Informationsaustausch adäquat zu ermöglichen. Schließlich müssen Dolmetscher auch die phraseologischen Elemente beherrschen, damit sie von den Zuhörern als Insider und letztendlich als fachkundig wahrgenommen werden.

Wenn Dolmetscher nicht selbst Fachleute in einem spezifischen Konferenzthema sind – was aufgrund der hohen kunden- und themenspezifischen Varianz sehr wahrscheinlich ist – müssen sie sich die drei aufgeführten Ebenen systematisch erschließen. In Anbetracht der Spontaneität und der zeitlichen Begrenzungen der im Dolmetschprozess stattfindenden Kommunikation ist es im Gegensatz zum Übersetzen notwendig, diesen Erschließungsprozess zu antizipieren, d.h. ihn in die Vorbereitungsphase zu verlagern (vgl. Gile 1995; Stoll 2009; Will 2009).

Um die Dolmetscher bei der Erschließung und Anwendung der drei genannten Wissensebenen zu unterstützen und generell die Rationalisierung des Dolmetschprozesses zu fördern, können Computeranwendungen eingesetzt werden. In den nachfolgenden Abschnitten werden die theoretischen Grundlagen zum Thema Terminologie- und Wissensmanagement im Bereich Dolmetschen kurz skizziert, die heute den Dolmetschern zur Verfügung stehenden Software analysiert und die möglichen Vorteile von korpuslinguistischen Ansätzen bei der Vorbereitung von Fachkonferenzen angesprochen. Im Anschluss daran wird schließlich eine Wissens- und Terminologie-Software namens InterpretBank vorgestellt, die speziell für Dolmetscher entwickelt wurde.

2 Wissen und Terminologie für Dolmetscher

Das Thema Wissens- und Terminologiemanagement sowie Einsatz von Computeranwendungen beim Dolmetschen hat erst in den letzten Jahren – wenn auch in geringem Maße – Eingang in die dolmetschwissenschaftliche Literatur gefunden. Um einen Überblick zu geben, werden in diesem Kapitel die wichtigsten Arbeiten zu diesen Themen chronologisch vorgestellt.

Fantinuoli (2006) fokussiert das terminologische Problem beim Dolmetschen auf die Notwendigkeit, qualitativ hochwertige sprachliche und nicht-sprachliche Ressourcen *ad-hoc* zu erstellen, da Dolmetscher aufgrund der Variabilität und Spezifität der von ihnen zu behandelnden Themen über keine vorgefertigten Ressourcen verfügen können. Dabei greift er auf computerlinguistische Anwendungen zurück und stellt den Ansatz der *Corpus Driven Interpreter Preparation* als Methode vor, um die in §1 genannten und für den Erfolg eines Dolmetscheinsatzes notwendigen Wissensebenen zu erschließen. Dieser Ansatz basiert auf dem

Gebrauch korpuslinguistischer Anwendungen, in erster Linie Software zur einsprachigen Konkordanzanalyse, die den Vorbereitungsprozess unterstützen sollen:

> To facilitate this process, we propose an approach to "Corpus Driven Interpreters Preparation". The process of "knowledge/language learning" needed by interpreters in order to prepare themselves for a conference can be optimized if "terminology driven", i.e., "bottom-up": from the terminology to the conceptual structure of a particular domain (Fantinuoli 2006: 174).

Da bei Konkordanzprogrammen ein Wort oder eine Phrase zur nächsten führen kann – abhängig von Intuition, Kompetenz, Interessen und Bedürfnissen eines Nutzers – können Korpora als Quelle eines unendlichen serendipity process (Johns 1988) betrachtet werden. Ausgehend von einer kleinen Anzahl an themenspezifischen Termini können Dolmetscher ein einsprachiges, themenspezifisches Fachkorpus „erforschen" und dabei lernen, wie sich ein Terminus innerhalb einer Domäne verhält, welche Bedeutungen er haben kann, etc. All dies geschieht mit einer „flexibility and active interaction typical of the interpreter's preparation" (Fantinuoli 2006: 174).

Rütten (2007) beschreibt den Terminologiebedarf der Dolmetscher als Teil des Informations- und Wissensmanagements im Bereich Konferenzdolmetschen und verfolgt das Ziel, die Rolle von Information und Wissen sowie entsprechende Zusammenhänge deutlich zu machen. Nachdem sie die wichtigsten Theorien dieser zwei Teildisziplinen näher beschreibt, schlägt sie eine Brücke zu den gängigen Dolmetschtheorien im Bereich Wissenskonstituierung wie z.B. zu den *Phasen* von Kalina (2005: 778) und plädiert für die Darstellung dieses Wissens nach Wüster (Rütten 2007: 83) anhand von Benennung, Begriff und Begriffsbeziehung. Die von ihr vorgeschlagene Darstellung von Zusammenhängen zwischen Dolmetschprozess und Wissen erläutert sie anhand einer Fallstudie, in der sie die Vorbereitungsarbeiten im Hinblick auf den informations- und wissensbezogenen Arbeitsablauf analysiert. Auf der Basis dieser Erkenntnisse schildert sie schließlich die Struktur eines Softwaremodells zur Unterstützung des Arbeitsablaufs.

Stoll (2009) beschreibt ein Modell der Vorverlagerung von Kognition aus der Phase des Simultandolmetschens in die Phase der Vorbereitung. Dabei tritt er für eine intensivere Auseinandersetzung mit dem Thema der Vorverlagerung des Denkaufwandes aus der Simultanphase ein, da sie zu einer Qualitätssteigerung führen kann. Er stützt sich dabei auf die in der Dolmetschwissenschaft anerkannte These, dass die fachliche Vorbereitung im Vorfeld stattfinden müsse und Dolmetscher in dieser Phase so viel Wissen wie möglich erwerben müssten (Gile

1995: 147), denn dies sei schließlich während der Konferenz nicht möglich. Dank der Vorverlagerung des kognitiven Aufwandes könnten Konzentrationsressourcen währen der Verdolmetschung freigesetzt werden, die dann z.B. auch für die Bedienung einer terminologischen Software während des Simultandolmetschens zur Verfügung stünden (Stoll 2002: 49).

Will (2009) setzt sich mit Modellen und Methoden auseinander, die notwendig sind, um die strukturellen Prozesse der Organisation terminologischer Arbeit für Dolmetscher zu definieren. Er beschreibt die komplexen Wissenskonstellationen, die für den Erfolg einer Dolmetschleistung grundlegend sind und entwickelt die in fünf Etappen zusammengefasste dolmetschorientierte Terminologiearbeit (DOT). Will bedient sich dabei des kontextspezifischen Terminus-Modells nach Gerzymisch-Arbogast (1996), das im Gegensatz zu Wüsters kontextunabhängiger, eindeutiger Zuordnung von Begriff und Bedeutung (Systemebene) auch die Möglichkeit von Abweichungen (Individualebene) vorsieht. Ausgehend von der Kritik an der Praxis, vor einem Dolmetscheinsatz einfache zusammenhanglose Wortlisten zu erstellen, die oft zu Fehlentscheidungen führen können, etwa wenn Polyseme oder Terminologisierungen auftreten (Will 2009: 6), plädiert Will für eine „Detektivarbeit", die – anders als bei punktuellen Glossaren – Wissen im Zusammenhang, d.h. im Kontext, abbildet. Bei dieser Detektivarbeit wird zunächst ein Wort (Benennung) als Begriff (Definition) erschlossen, um zu erkennen, welchem Wissensbereich der Terminus zugeordnet werden kann (vgl. Will 2010). Nur so könne eine sichere und adäquate Verdolmetschung ermöglicht werden.

In seiner Arbeit über terminologische Probleme beim Medizindolmetschen konstatiert Gorjanic schließlich, wie „Communication problems often arise from insufficient knowledge of terminology rather than a lack of general language skills" (Gorjanc 2009: 85). Er geht von Fantinuoli (2006) These zur Ressourcenknappheit aus und behauptet, dass Dolmetscher Strategien entwickeln müssen, um Datenbestände für das jeweilige Thema selbst zu erarbeiten. Dies kann durch spezialisierte Anwendungen zur Vorbereitung und Analyse sprachlicher Ressourcen sowie zur Speicherung und Verwaltung der Ergebnisse eines solchen Verfahrens erzielt werden. Aus dieser Notwendigkeit heraus kommt er zu dem Schluss, „the educational process includes information on terminology management options based on text resources" (Gorjanc 2009: 89).

3 Nutzungsverbreitung von Computeranwendungen unter den Dolmetschern

Seit den 90er Jahren wurden unter Konferenzdolmetschern zahlreiche Umfragen zu deren Erfahrung mit dem Computereinsatz in ihrem dolmetschbezogenen

Berufsleben durchgeführt. All diese Umfragen hatten zum Ziel, die Verbreitung von Programmen zur Terminologieverwaltung zu analysieren. Die in den letzten Jahren durchgeführten Umfragen (vgl. Valentini 2002; Honegger 2006; Sprachen and Dolmetscher Institut München 2007; Bilgen 2009) zeigen hinsichtlich der Verbreitung der für Dolmetscher entwickelten Werkzeuge ein ernüchterndes Bild. Für die Terminologieverwaltung verwenden die meisten Befragten – wenn überhaupt – immer noch traditionelle Lösungen wie z.B. Textverarbeitungs- und Tabellenkalkulationsprogramme (z.B. *MS-Word* oder *MS-Excel*); nur selten werden Programme verwendet, die auch eine Simultanmodalität besitzen. Keiner der Befragten erwähnt korpuslinguistische Anwendungen, wie beispielsweise Konkordanz-Software, Tools zur Korpuserstellung, Terminologieextraktion, Wissenserschließung, etc. Dennoch zeichnet sich seit einigen Jahren ein stetig wachsendes Interesse für Methoden und praktische Anwendungen ab, die die Vorbereitung, Durchführung und Nachbearbeitung eines Dolmetscheinsatzes effizienter gestalten sollten. Das wachsende Interesse spiegelt sich auch in der Zahl dolmetschwissenschaftlicher Publikationen wider (siehe §2), die zu diesem Thema veröffentlicht wurden.

4 Ressourcen und Tools für Dolmetscher

Es ist allgemein bekannt, dass das Internet die vertrauteste und nutzerfreundlichste Arbeitsumgebung für Übersetzer und Dolmetscher ist (Zanettin 2002). Man kann zu Recht davon ausgehen, dass alle Dolmetscher und Übersetzer heutzutage das Medium Internet als wichtigste Quelle für die Beschaffung von Informationen und Terminologie zu einem bestimmten Thema nutzen. Internetsuchmaschinen bieten in erster Linie die Möglichkeit, eine fast unendliche Menge an ein- oder mehrsprachigen Texten über alle erdenklichen Fachgebiete zu finden, die – zusammen mit den konferenzspezifischen Texten, die vom Konferenzorganisator oder *Chef d'équipe* zur Verfügung gestellt werden – als Grundlage für die Vorbereitung einer Konferenz dienen. Dabei geht es um Paralleltexte, d.h. thematisch verwandte Texte in der Zielsprache, die zur Erschließung linguistischer und nicht-linguistischer Elemente verwendet werden können, wie z.B. die Suche nach Äquivalenten eines Terminus in einer anderen Sprache. Das Internet bietet darüber hinaus zahlreiche, oft kostenlose Möglichkeiten, strukturierte Informationen zu einem bestimmten Thema zu finden. Dies ist beispielsweise bei allgemeinen Enzyklopädien wie Wikipedia[3] der Fall, wo Einträge zu einer nahezu unbegrenzten Anzahl von Themen enthalten sind, oder bei fachspezifischen

---

[3] http://www.wikipedia.org

Ressourcen wie z.B. der Wissensdatenbank Phenowiki[4], die Informationen über psychiatrische Erscheinungen zum Inhalt hat. Auch die Anzahl der terminologischen und lexikografischen Ressourcen – sowohl ein- als auch mehrsprachige – ist sehr groß. Man denke nur an terminologische Datenbanken wie IATE[5], die mehrsprachige Terminologie-Datenbank der EU, kollaborative Internetseiten zur Speicherung von Übersetzungen wie Leo[6], oder lexikografische Ressourcen wie DWDS[7].

Anders als das Internet, das immer mehr Ressourcen bietet, die für Dolmetscher und Übersetzer nützlich sind, ist die Anzahl der dolmetschspezifischen Software – im Gegensatz zur Übersetzungsbranche, in der sich viele Software zur Unterstützung des Übersetzungsprozesses etabliert haben – in Zahl, Funktionsumfang und Verbreitung sehr begrenzt. Die Gründe hierfür sind vielfältig. Einerseits ist der Konferenzmarkt im Vergleich zum Übersetzungsmarkt wesentlich kleiner (kleinere Anzahl der praktizierenden Dolmetscher und kleinere Auftragsvolumina), so dass das wirtschaftliche Interesse der Softwarehersteller sehr gering ist. Andererseits fehlt das Bewusstsein seitens der Dolmetscher, dass durch ein besseres Management der zur Verfügung stehenden Ressourcen eine höhere Wettbewerbsfähigkeit und eine bessere Qualität der erbrachten Leistungen erzielt werden können. Dies könnte an den „schwer erfassbaren Arbeitsbedingungen, unter denen Dolmetscher mit Texten konfrontiert werden" (Will 2009: 19) liegen.

Die meisten dolmetschspezifischen Software, die im Laufe der Jahre entwickelt wurden, sind rein terminologische Datenbanken: Sie dienen ausschließlich der Speicherung und Verwaltung mehrsprachiger Glossare. Im Gegensatz zu den Terminologiesystemen für Übersetzer zeichnen sie sich meistens durch eine vereinfachte Eintragsstruktur und durch die Implementierung einer Funktionalität zum Abrufen der Glossare in der Kabine aus (ähnlich wie bei den elektronischen Wörterbüchern). Zu den Lösungen, die für Dolmetscher entwickelt wurden, gehören Interplex[8], Terminus[9], Lookup[10] und TermDB[11]. Alle Lösungen ermöglichen das Anlegen und die Verwaltung mehrsprachiger Wortlisten und bieten Felder für

---

[4] http://www.phenowiki.org
[5] http://www.iate.europa.eu
[6] http://www.leo.de
[7] http://www.dwds.de
[8] http://www.fourwillows.com/interplex
[9] http://www.terminus.wintringham.ch
[10] http://www.lookup-web.de/
[11] TermDB wurde von einem AIIC-Konferenzdolmetscher entwickelt und nie kommerziell vertrieben.

das Eintragen von Zusatzinformationen. Außer der Einteilung in Glossaren bieten sie – mit Ausnahme von Interplex – einige weitere Kategorisierungsmöglichkeiten wie z.B. Konferenz, Thema oder Kundenzuordnung. Die Suche nach einem Wort erfolgt meist durch Eingabe einer Zeichenkette in das Suchfeld und durch Drücken der Eingabetaste. Keine der oben genannten Software nutzt allerdings computerlinguistische Ansätze, um die Suchfunktion kabinenfreundlicher zu gestalten. So ermöglicht keine dieser Software in der uns vorliegenden Version eine Reduzierung der Trefferquote z.B. durch Stopwords oder durch eine Fehlerkorrektur im Falle eines Tippfehlers/Rechtschreibfehlers im Glossar; beide sind allerdings wichtige Eigenschaften für die *Usability* einer simultanfähigen Software (siehe §6.3).

Einige Sprachendienste internationaler Unternehmen oder Institutionen haben im Laufe der Jahre eigene Lösungen entwickelt. Eine erwähnenswerte Anwendung für Dolmetscher ist Lithos, die terminologische Software der Generaldirektion Dolmetschen der Europäischen Union. Anders als bei den oben genannten Programmen handelt es sich bei Lithos um eine Server-Client-Anwendung zur Verwaltung und Bereitstellung mehrsprachiger Glossare, die von den fest angestellten und freiberuflichen Dolmetschern der EU eingesetzt werden kann. Lithos liegt eine Datenbank zugrunde, die alle 24 EU-Amtssprachen umfasst. Des Weiteren sind Felder zur thematischen Einordnung der Einträge und deren Zuweisung zu einem bestimmten Glossar vorgesehen. Die auf einem zentralen Server gespeicherte Datenbank von Lithos wird monatlich durch Ergänzung der zuletzt vom SCIC-Terminologiedienst veröffentlichten Glossare aktualisiert. Abgesehen vom direkten Online-Zugang über einen Internetbrowser unterstützt Lithos die Installation eines Clients auf dem Rechner des Nutzers zur Anwendung der Datenbank im Offline-Modus. Die Offline-Datenbank kann jederzeit aktualisiert und somit auf den Stand der Online-Version gebracht werden.

5 Computer- und Korpuslinguistik in der Dolmetschpraxis

Im Gegensatz zu allgemeinen und dolmetschspezifischen Programmen zur Terminologieverwaltung, die unter Dolmetschern heutzutage einen gewissen Bekanntheitsgrad erreicht haben, haben korpuslinguistische Ansätze bis heute so gut wie keine Resonanz im Bereich des Dolmetschens gefunden. Einzige Ausnahme stellt die deskriptive Dolmetschwissenschaft dar, die seit einigen Jahren mit den so genannten *Corpus-Based Interpreting Studies* nach Erkenntnissen über unterschiedlichste Aspekte des Dolmetschens sucht. Einige Beispiele dafür sind Studien zur

Direktionalität beim Simultandolmetschen (Bendazzoli & Sandrelli 2005), zu Strategien beim Simultan- und Konsekutivdolmetschen in Bezug auf Eigennamen (Meyer 2008), oder zu den Implikationen des Einsatzes nicht professioneller Dolmetscher im Gesundheitswesen (Meyer u. a. 2010). Die Gründe für die zeitliche Verzögerung des Einzugs der Korpuslinguistik in die Dolmetschpraxis und in die Dolmetscherausbildung sind vielfältig. Mit wenigen Ausnahmen (Fantinuoli 2006; Gorjanc 2009) hat sich die Dolmetschwissenschaft einerseits noch nicht mit den Möglichkeiten auseinandergesetzt, die die Computer- und Korpuslinguistik für die Praxis des Dolmetschens und für die Ausbildung angehender Dolmetscher bietet; andererseits fehlen spezifische computerlinguistische Anwendungen, die genau auf die Bedürfnisse der Dolmetscher zugeschnitten sind. Die Computer- und Korpuslinguistik kann für die Dolmetschpraxis und -ausbildung jedoch einen wichtigen Beitrag leisten. Bei angehenden Dolmetschern können Lernerkorpora, zum Beispiel aus politischen Reden, Antworten zu den sprachlichen Besonderheiten dieser Sprache liefern, vor allem in Bezug auf die Verdolmetschung in die Fremdsprache. Der Lerner wird somit emanzipiert und die Lernautonomie gefördert. Bei professionellen Dolmetschern kann sie insbesondere für eine Optimierung der Vorbereitungsphase sorgen, indem sie gezielte Informationen und Darstellungsformen zu einem bestimmten Fachthema bereitstellt. Die gewonnenen sprachlichen und nicht-sprachlichen Daten können systematisiert und für zukünftige Projekte wiederverwendet werden, was die Wirtschaftlichkeit der einzelnen Dolmetscheinsätze langfristig erhöht (siehe §6).

Um die Bedeutung eines Fachterminus besser zu verstehen und diesen korrekt und nutzeradäquat zu verwenden, ist es zum Beispiel möglich, aus einem themenspezifischen einsprachigen Fachkorpus reelle Verwendungsbeispiele zu visualisieren. Die Einbeziehung der aktuellen Realisierung von Termini und Phrasen in Originaltexten ist die Voraussetzung dafür, dass „Termini im Kontext beschrieben und mit ihrer Systembedeutung verglichen werden können" (Will 2009: 42). Das Nachschlagen in Parallelkorpora kann darüber hinaus eine unerschöpfliche Quelle an Übersetzungsvorschlägen sein. Für diese Art der Informationsgewinnung aus Korpora eignet sich die klassische Form der Darstellung von korpuslinguistischen Befunden, das so genannte *Key Words in Context*. Die geordnete Darstellung von Konkordanzen ermöglicht es dem Nutzer, zu neuen Erkenntnissen über Sprache und Inhalt zu gelangen. Der Prozess der Korpusanalyse kann außerdem dazu beitragen, vorhandene Kenntnisse zu verfestigen (Johns 1991) und erscheint somit geeignet, Dolmetscher vor einem Dolmetscheinsatz bei der Aktivierung ihres Vorwissens zu unterstützen (siehe §2). Die Wichtigkeit dieser „contextual patterns" (Aston 2001: 15) im Bereich der aktiven Sprachbeherrschung wird in vielen wissenschaftlichen Arbeiten thematisiert.[12] Hier ist auch die Kernidee der *Corpus Driven Interpreter Preparation* (Fantinuoli 2006) angesiedelt. Ergänzt durch weitere Informationen inhaltlicher und sprachlicher Natur (siehe §6.1.4), die auf einer zentralen Benutzeroberfläche dargestellt werden, kann die Analyse eines Fachkorpus dazu beitragen, die drei in §2 definierten Wissensebenen zu erlangen. Dies wird ermöglicht, indem das Korpus und die Konkordanzen als Quellen für einen unendlichen *serendipity process* (Johns 1988) benutzt werden, da ein Wort zum nächsten führt, abhängig von Intuition, Kenntnissen, Interessen und Bedarf des Nutzers (Bernardini 2001). Dieser Ansatz findet offensichtlich auch bei Will Zuspruch, denn er konstatiert:

> Diese Detektivarbeit ist deswegen von Bedeutung, weil sie [...] Wissen im Zusammenhang abbildet, wobei dieser Zusammenhang auf weitere Termini, auch aus verschiedenen Texten, ausgeweitet werden kann und sollte (Will 2010: 53).

Ähnlich wie beim Spracherwerb steht die Verwendung von Korpora in der Dolmetschvorbereitungsphase im Einklang mit dem klassischen affektiven Prinzip des emotionalen und nicht nur rationalen Lernansatzes, der in den letzten Jahren im Mittelpunkt des wissenschaftlichen Diskurses im Bereich des fremdsprachlichen Spracherwerbs stand (Balboni 2002: 240).

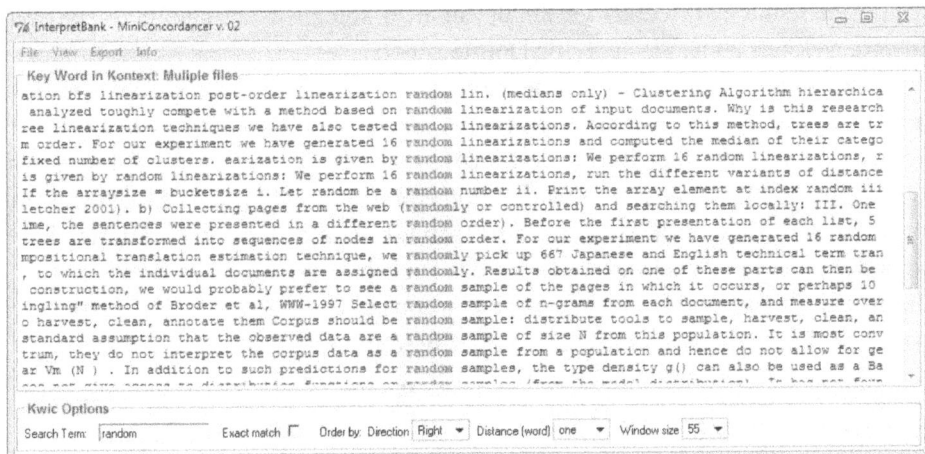

Abbildung 1: Einsprachige Konkordanzen

Im Bereich Spracherwerb und Übersetzungsdidaktik ist die Hauptidee, den Lernenden in ein aktives Mitglied des Lernprozesses zu verwandeln (Kiraly 2000)

---

[12] Eine ausführliche Einführung bietet hierzu Aston (2001).

und den Lernprozess datenbasiert anstatt regelbasiert zu gestalten. In diesem Zusammenhang beschreibt Boulton das Data Driven Learning (DDL) mit folgenden Worten:

> DDL typically involves exposing learners to large quantities of authentic data – the electronic corpus – so that they can play an active role in exploring the language and detecting patterns in it. They are at the centre of the process, taking increased responsibility for their own learning rather than being taught rules in a more passive mode (2009: 82).

DDL steht wiederum im Einklang mit dem Spracherwerbsansatz von Johns (1994). Seiner These nach können die Merkmale einer Sprache mittels eines Konkordanzprogramms und der daraus resultierenden Arbeit mit echten Verwendungsbeispielen erlernt werden. Das Experimentieren mit Korpora bietet "virtually unlimited opportunities for learning by discovery, as learners embark on challenging journeys whose outcomes are unpredictable and usually rewarding" (Bernardini 2001: 246). Der Lerner wird somit zur Hauptfigur des Lernprozesses. Bei der Einsatzvorbereitung kann der Dolmetscher ähnlich wie der Sprachlerner eine größere Autonomie bei der Suche und Verifizierung der eigenen Übersetzungsvorschläge erlangen. Korpora können in der Tat eine hilfreiche Quelle für Terminologie und faktische Informationen sein. Dies gilt sowohl für Übersetzer (Friedbichler & Friedbichler 2000; Zanettin 2002; Castagnoli 2006; Hansen-Schirra & Teich 2008) als auch für Dolmetscher.

Nachdem die ersten theoretischen Arbeiten im Bereich linguistischer und extra-linguistischer Vorbereitungsstrategien professioneller Dolmetscher erschienen sind,[13] die etwas Licht auf den terminologischen Bedarf der Dolmetscher geworfen haben, wurde der Versuch unternommen, ein korpuslinguistisches Instrumentarium für diese Zielgruppe zu entwickeln und zu implementieren. Dies ist das Ziel des Projekts InterpretBank, das am Fachbereich Translations-, Sprach- und Kulturwissenschaft der Johannes Gutenberg-Universität Mainz entwickelt wurde und das im nächsten Kapitel näher beschrieben wird.

6 IntepretBank

InterpretBank[14] ist ein modulares Tool, welches die Dolmetscher im Bereich Wissens- und Terminologiemanagement vor, während und nach einem Einsatz un-

---

[13] Hierzu die *Corpus Driven Interpreter Preparation* von Fantinuoli (2006) und die *Dolmetschorientierte Terminologiearbeit* von Will (2009).

[14] www.interpretbank.com

terstützt. Dabei wird besonders viel Wert auf die Vorbereitungsphase gelegt. Diese spielt bei jedem Dolmetscheinsatz eine entscheidende Rolle: Einerseits beeinflusst sie maßgeblich die Qualität der Dolmetschleistung (Kalina 2005: 777), andererseits hängt die Wirtschaftlichkeit eines Einsatzes von der Zeit ab, die in die Vorbereitung investiert wird.

> Insbesondere die Betrachtungen zur Optimierung basieren auf der Annahme, dass der Dolmetscher als homo oeconomicus bzw. Unternehmen agiert. Das heißt, er betreibt das Dolmetschen nicht als Hobby, bei dem es ihm erlaubt wäre, unbegrenzt viel Zeit in die Vorbereitung und Nachbereitung eines Dolmetscheinsatzes zu stecken, sondern ist bestrebt, seine Ressourcen optimal, also kosteneffizient einzusetzen, was ihn bestimmten – zeitlichen und finanziellen – Zwängen unterwirft (Rütten 2007: 5 ff).

Die Frage der Wirtschaftlichkeit lässt sich einfach erklären, wenn man bedenkt, dass z.B. auf dem freien Markt die Vorbereitungszeit in der Regel pauschal mit dem vereinbarten Tagessatz honoriert wird; d.h. der tatsächliche Vorbereitungsaufwand spielt bei der Setzung des Tageshonorars nur eine untergeordnete Rolle. Je länger ein Dolmetscher sich auf einen Einsatz vorbereiten muss, desto unwirtschaftlicher wird sein Einsatz. Rein ökonomisch betrachtet, würde diese Überlegung für eine Verkürzung der Vorbereitungsphase sprechen. Dagegen spricht jedoch die Notwendigkeit, eine qualitativ hochwertige Leistung zu erbringen, und diese erfordert wiederum einen beachtlichen Zeitaufwand für die Vorbereitung. Das Verhältnis Wirtschaftlichkeit/Qualität kann verbessert werden, indem man die von den Dolmetschern angewandten Strategien der Vorbereitung rationalisiert und optimiert. Die Vorverlagerung der kognitiven Prozesse auf die Zeit vor der Konferenz entlastet den Dolmetscher während der Verdolmetschung selbst. Durch diese Entlastung können Dolmetscher besser auf Software zugreifen wie z.B. Abrufsysteme für die Konferenzterminologie (Stoll 2002). Diese ermöglichen es ihnen wiederum, die Qualität der erbrachten Leistung weiter zu erhöhen.

Um dies zu ermöglichen, bietet InterpretBank folgende Module, die auf den in der Dolmetschwissenschaft beschriebenen Phasen eines Konferenzeinsatzes (Kalina 2005: 778; Will 2009: 52ff) basieren:

- *CorpusMode*: Modul zur Konferenzvorbereitung durch automatische Termextraktion sowie Informationssuche aus automatisch hergestellten Fachkorpora und aus strukturierten Webquellen

- *TermMode*: Modul zur Erstellung und Pflege der Terminologiebestände

- *ConferenceMode*: Modul zum Nachschlagen von Glossaren während des Simultaneinsatzes

Die Module zielen darauf ab, alle Phasen eines Dolmetscheinsatzes computertechnisch zu unterstützen, von der Vorbereitung (*CorpusMode*) bis hin zur Konferenz (*ConferenceMode*). Mit Ausnahme des TreeTaggers wurde InterpretBank komplett in der Programmiersprache Perl[15] für Windows geschrieben und steht für nicht kommerzielle Zwecke kostenlos zur Verfügung[16].

6.1 Zur Vorbereitung des Einsatzes: CorpusMode

Wie in §2 beschrieben, spielt die Vorbereitungsphase einer Fachkonferenz in einem den Dolmetschern noch nicht bekannten Fachgebiet eine entscheidende Rolle. In dieser Phase müssen sich Dolmetscher eine Reihe von Informationen sprachlicher und inhaltlicher Natur aneignen, die notwendig sind, um einen Dolmetscheinsatz erfolgreich durchführen zu können.

CorpusMode bündelt linguistische und extra-linguistische Informationen zu einem bestimmten Konferenzthema in eine einzige graphische Benutzeroberfläche. Dabei werden alle drei in §2 aufgeführten Schlüsselkompetenzbereiche abgedeckt: Inhalt, Terminologie und Phraseologie. Das Modul soll es Dolmetschern ermöglichen, sich gezielt nach dem Prinzip der *Corpus Driven Interpreter Preparation* (Fantinuoli 2006) vorzubereiten. Dies geschieht durch die automatische Bereitstellung unterschiedlicher konferenzrelevanter Informationen, die in den folgenden Kapiteln näher beschrieben werden.

Der Workflow von CorpusMode beginnt mit der automatischen Sammlung relevanter Texte aus dem Internet zum Konferenzthema (§6.1.1). Aus dem erstellten Korpus wird die Fachterminologie extrahiert (§6.1.2), Definitionen und Übersetzungskandidaten zu jedem Terminus werden aus ausgewählten Quellen im Internet übernommen (§6.1.4), verwandte Wörter und Kollokationen werden ermittelt (§6.1.5). All diese Informationen werden schließlich auf einer integrierten Benutzeroberfläche (Abb. 2) angezeigt. Darüber hinaus bietet CorpusMode die Möglichkeit, Konkordanzen aus dem erstellten einsprachigen Korpus und aus frei verfügbaren Parallelkorpora zu analysieren (siehe §6.1.3). Die Informationen, die mit CorpusMode erschlossen wurden, können anschließend mit dem eigenen terminologischen Werkzeug, TermMode, fixiert und für den späteren Gebrauch archiviert werden.

---

[15] www.activestate.com
[16] www.interpretbank.de

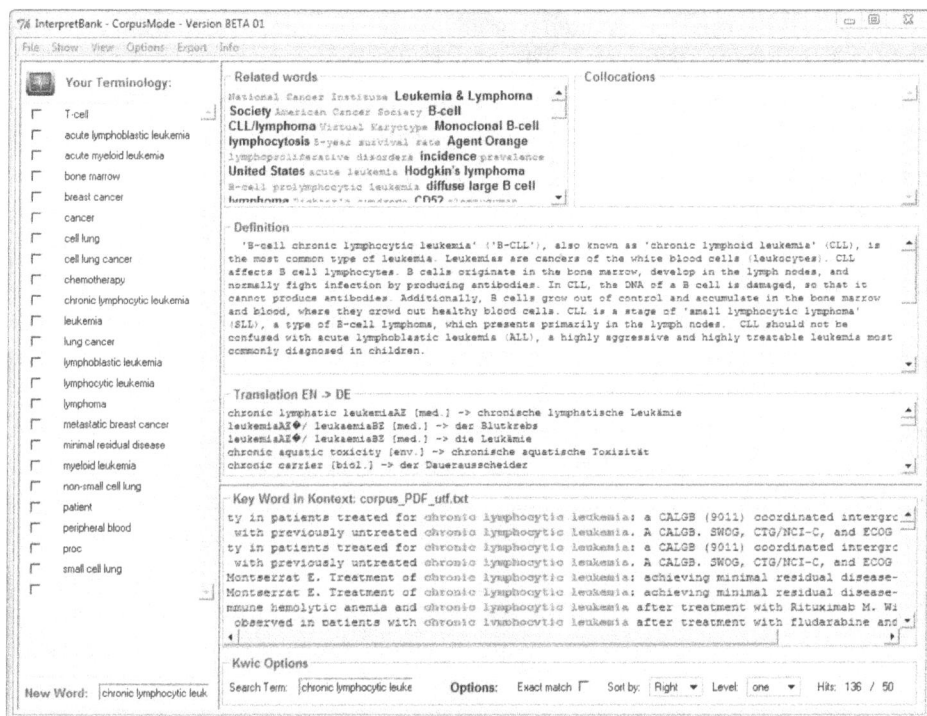

Abbildung 2: Benutzeroberfläche von CorpusMode

6.1.1 Automatische Erstellung einsprachiger Fachkorpora

CorpusMode sammelt automatisch fachspezifische, konferenzrelevante Texte –
die so genannten Paralleltexte – aus dem Web und erstellt ein Fachkorpus. Die
Idee, das Internet als Quelle für die Erstellung von Korpora zu verwenden, ist
nicht neu und seit einigen Jahren Thema zahlreicher wissenschaftlicher Arbeiten
(Ghani, Jones & Mladenic 2001; Baroni & Bernardini 2004):

> The Web is immense, free, and available by mouse click. It contains hund-
> reds of billions of words of text and can be used for all manner of language
> research (Kilgarriff & Grefenstette 2003: 333).

Das Internet kann als eine fast unendliche und leicht zugängliche Quelle linguistischer Daten betrachtet werden, die sehr gut geeignet ist, um *disposable*[17]

---

[17] Zur Bedeutung von *Disposable Corpora* Varantola (2003).

Korpora „on-the-run" zu erstellen, vor allem Fachkorpora, die einmalig oder nur im Rahmen eines Projektes – sprich einer Konferenz – Verwendung finden[18].

Die grundlegende Funktionsweise ist einfach und basiert auf dem Ansatz von BootCaT (Baroni & Bernardini 2004): Das Thema des Fachkorpus, welches gleichzeitig Konferenzthema ist, wird durch fünf oder sechs Termini festgelegt, die für die Konferenz relevant sind – beispielsweise durch die Begriffe *leukemia, bone marrow, chemotherapy, transplantation and acute lymphoblastic leukemia* bei einer Konferenz über *Acute Leukemia*. Diese werden miteinander kombiniert und als Suchwörter bei einer Suchmaschine, in unserem Fall Bing[19], verwendet. Die von der Suchmaschine gefundenen PDF-Dokumente[20] werden heruntergeladen und als Text formatiert. Das Resultat dieses Prozesses ist ein einsprachiges Korpus, das Texte beinhaltet, die inhaltlich mit den Suchwörtern verwandt sind.[21] Als Quelle für diese Suchwörter können z.B. Konferenzprogramme dienen bzw. die Titel der einzelnen Vorträge oder Abstracts, die von den einzelnen Referenten gehalten werden und die meist schon einige Zeit vor der Konferenz zur Verfügung stehen. Um diesen Prozess noch weiter zu beschleunigen, können sich Dolmetscher dem Konferenzthema auch annähern, indem sie ein einziges Wort eingeben, das das Konferenzthema am allgemeinsten bezeichnet, z.B. *solar energy, semiconductor* oder *circuit design*. CorpusMode erstellt daraufhin nach der in §6.1.5 beschriebenen Methode automatisch eine Liste verwandter Wörter. Diese Termini werden dann als Suchwörter für die Suchmaschinenabfrage verwendet.

Vorteile dieser Methode, Korpora zu jedem beliebigen Thema automatisch zu erstellen, sind die Einfachheit und Schnelligkeit. In wenigen Minuten können Korpora mit hunderttausenden von Tokens erstellt werden. Nachteile sind dagegen die kaum vorhandenen Möglichkeiten der Kontrolle der gefundenen Texte. Unterschiedliche Tests haben jedoch ergeben, dass die Qualität der hergestellten Fachkorpora für die *Corpus Driven Interpreter Preparation* sehr zufriedenstellend ist (Fantinuoli 2006). Die Qualität hängt im Wesentlichen von der Auswahl der Suchwörter ab und kann somit vom Benutzter gesteuert werden (Ueyama 2006). Die Möglichkeit, die gefundenen Texte auf Relevanz und Qualität zu überprüfen, ist dennoch gegeben.

Eine weitere Methode zur Erstellung eines Fachkorpus ist die kleine Software CorpusCreator, die ebenfalls Teil von InterpretBank ist. Mit dieser Software ist

---

[18] Zur Differenzierung von den unterschiedlichen Korporatypologien vgl. Hansen-Schirra & Teich (2008) und Lemnitzer & Zinsmeister (2010).

[19] ww.bing.com

[20] Dabei werden die erweiterten Suchoptionen für die Suche nach bestimmten Formaten verwendet, in unserem Fall PDF-Dateien

[21] Vgl. die Methode von BootCaT in Baroni & Bernardini (2004).

es möglich, Korpora aus PDF-Dateien auf der Grundlage einer Suchmaschinen-Suche zu erstellen.[22] Der Nutzer benutzt z.B. die Suchmaschine Google und ihre leistungsfähige erweiterte Suche, um relevante Texte zu einem bestimmten Thema zu finden. Um ein englisches Korpus zum Thema Solarenergie zu erstellen, kann man zum Beispiel themenverwandte PDF-Dateien mit der folgenden Query finden: „solar cells filetype:pdf site:.com"[23]. Um ein deutsches Korpus über die Unternehmenssprache der Firma Gehrlicher AG zu erstellen, ist es möglich folgende Query zu benutzten: „filetype:pdf site:gehrlicher.com". Die Internetseite mit den Suchergebnis wird als HTML-Datei auf der Festplatte des Nutzers gespeichert und von CorpusCreator verwendet, um alle gefundene PDF-Dateien automatisch herunterzuladen und in Text-Format zu konvertieren.

Die semi-automatisch erstellten Korpora werden für die Abfrage durch einen *Concordancer* vorbereitet. Zuerst werden sie mit Metadaten angereichert. Das Markup enthält Informationen zu den Original-Dateien (Titel der Datei, URL, Timestamp, Kodierung, etc.). Dabei wird auf ein einfaches XML-Schema zurückgegriffen:

(1)
```
<header>
    <filename></filename>
    <url></url>
    <\isi{encoding}></\isi{encoding}>
    <conversionTime></conversionTime>
</header>
```

Das Korpus wird linguistisch mit morphosyntaktischen Merkmalen (Part-of-Speech Tagging) annotiert. Hierfür wird ein POS-Tagger[24] verwendet, d.h. eine Software, die in der Lage ist, jedes Token eines Textes einer bestimmten Wortklasse zuzuweisen. Auf weitere linguistische Annotationsebenen (syntaktische Annotation, semantische Annotation, Lemmatisierung, usw.) wird dagegen verzichtet, da diese in der Regel sehr zeitaufwendig ist und nur mit einem beträchtlichen manuellen Aufwand durchgeführt werden können. Die Flüchtigkeit der erstellten Korpora, die oft nur für einen einzigen Dolmetscheinsatz Verwendung finden, macht diese aufwendigen Annotationen unwirtschaftlich. Die Korpusabfrage erfolgt auf der Grundlage von Wortformen. Diese ist insbesondere für lexi-

---

[22] Dabei kann eine beliebige Suchmaschine verwendet werden. Die hier angeführten Beispiele beruhen auf Suchvorgängen mit Google.

[23] In Google begrenzt *filetype* die Suche auf ein bestimmtes Dateiformat, *site* auf eine bestimmte Internetdomäne.

[24] Es wird der TreeTagger verwendet (www.ims.uni-stuttgart.de/projekte/corplex/TreeTagger)

kografische Fragestellungen geeignet. Um die Abfrage zu unterspezifizieren, um zum Beispiel gleichzeitig nach verschiedenen Flexionsformen zu suchen, ist es möglich, nicht nur nach Wortformen zu suchen, sondern über reguläre Ausdrücke eine Mustersuche (wie z.B. Alteration, Gruppierung, Zeichenklasse, usw.) durchzuführen.[25]

6.1.2 Automatische Extraktion von Fachterminologie

Die Fachterminologie einer Konferenz wird aus dem Fachkorpus (§6.1.1) automatisch extrahiert. Die implementierte Extraktionsmethode basiert auf statistischen und linguistischen Ansätzen, die in einem Hybridverfahren kombiniert werden. Der statistische Ansatz beruht auf dem Vergleich der relativen Häufigkeit eines Tokens im Fachkorpus mit der relativen Häufigkeit desselben Tokens in einem Vergleichskorpus (Rayson & Gariside 2000). Anhand dreier unterschiedlicher statistischer Verfahren – *Weirdness Ratio*, *Log Likelihood Ratio* und *Log Odds Ratio*– werden die typischen Tokens des Fachkorpus, also Einworttermini, identifiziert. Exemplarisch wird hier der Wert von der *Weirdness Ratio* eines Tokens errechnet:

$$Weirdness\,Ratio = (Wspec/Tspec)/(Wref/Tref)$$

Wspec = Häufigkeit des Tokens x im Fachkorpus

Wref = Häufigkeit des Tokens x im Referenzkorpus

Tspec = Anzahl aller Token im Fachkorpus

Tref = Anzahl aller Token im Referenzkorpus

Aus dieser Formel ist ersichtlich, dass die *Weirdness Ratio* einen höheren Wert haben wird, wenn die relative Häufigkeit des Tokens im Fachkorpus höher als im Referenzkorpus ist. Dies kann als Indikator dafür betrachtet werden, dass das Token typisch für das Fachkorpus ist.

Alle Tokens aus dem Fachkorpus werden schließlich in eine einzige Rangfolge gesetzt, indem man die Rangfolgen aus jedem einzelnen statistischen Verfahren miteinander kombiniert.[26] Um die Qualität der extrahierten Einworttermini zu verbessern, wird außerdem die zuvor durchgeführte morphosyntaktische Analyse verwendet. Die Einworttermini, die statistisch identifiziert wurden, werden

---

[25] Für weitere Details zu den *regular expressions* siehe Friedl (2006).

[26] Vgl. das sogenannte „rank aggregation problem" (Dwork u. a. 2001).

nun anhand von POS-Filtern selektiert. Somit können einzelne Wortklassen herausausgefiltert werden. In der Regel werden Substantive ausgewählt, da diese terminologisch am relevantesten sind. Die Möglichkeit, auch weitere Wortklassen zu extrahieren, z.B. Verben oder Adjektive, bleibt jedoch ebenso gewahrt.

Mehrworttermini werden durch ein linguistisches Verfahren ermittelt. Aus dem mit POS-Tags angereicherten Korpus werden nach festgelegten Wortklassenmustern, wie z.B. für die englische Sprache „Noun + Noun", „Adjective + Noun" oder „Noun + Noun + Noun", alle Mehrworttermini extrahiert, die den vorgegebenen Mustern entsprechen. Statistisch bereinigt wird diese Liste durch die Errechnung der relativen Häufigkeit dieser Kandidaten im Fachkorpus in Bezug auf deren Häufigkeit im Referenzkorpus. Das Ergebnis der Extraktion ist eine Liste von Einwort- und Mehrworttermkandidaten.

Die Bewertung der Qualität einer automatischen Terminologieextraktion ist von ihrer Zielsetzung abhängig. Aus diesem Grund werden die Anzahl und der Typ der Termkandidaten, die in der Benutzeroberfläche angezeigt werden, nicht vorab festgelegt, sondern dem Nutzer überlassen. Damit die Software den unterschiedlichen terminologischen Bedürfnissen des Nutzers Rechnung tragen kann, ist es möglich, anhand eines sogenannten TerminologyEqualizers die Charakteristika der zu extrahierenden Termini zu bestimmen und somit die Zielsetzung der Extraktion anzupassen; beispielsweise können sich Benutzer nur hochspezifische Termini anzeigen lassen oder hochspezifische Termini plus allgemeinere Termini; nur Substantive oder Substantive plus Verben und Adjektive; usw. Durch diese Anpassbarkeit der Terminologieextraktion können Dolmetscher – je nach Vorkenntnissen oder je nach den Sprachen, mit denen sie arbeiten müssen – selbst entscheiden, welche Termini sie für eine optimale Vorbereitung des Einsatzes benötigen (Fantinuoli 2006). Die Termextraktion wurde bis dato für die Sprachen English, Deutsch und Italienisch implementiert. Da die sprachlichen Ressourcen (z.B. die Parameterdateien des TreeTaggers) auch für andere Sprachen vorhanden sind, kann die Implementierung mit relativ geringem Aufwand auf andere Sprachen ausgeweitet werden.

6.1.3 Einbindung von Parallelkorpora

Eine weitere Möglichkeit, dolmetschrelevante Informationen aus Textsammlungen zu gewinnen, besteht in der Untersuchung von Parallelkorpora, in denen Originaltexte ihren Übersetzungen in eine oder mehrere Zielsprachen zugeordnet sind. Diese werden generell benutzt, um Terminologie (Pearson 2003), Kollokationen (Teubert 2003) und Valenzen (Čulo 2011) automatisch oder manuell zu extrahieren. Beim professionellen Übersetzen und Dolmetschen können Parallelkorpora die Zahl der zur Verfügung stehenden sprachlichen Ressourcen ergänzen und vervollständigen.

> A parallel corpus can be employed as a multilingual lexical resource, being more comprehensive and diverse than dictionaries (Hansen-Schirra & Teich 2008: 1168).

Eine der wichtigsten Eigenschaften von Parallelkorpora ist die Tatsache, dass die Originaltexte satzweise mit den Zieltexten aligniert sind, d.h. die Textteile (Sätze, Absätze, usw.) werden einander zugeordnet. Dies ermöglicht u.a. die parallele Darstellung vom Ausgangs- und Zieltext in einer für die manuelle Informationsgewinnung nützlichen Form (Abb. 3).

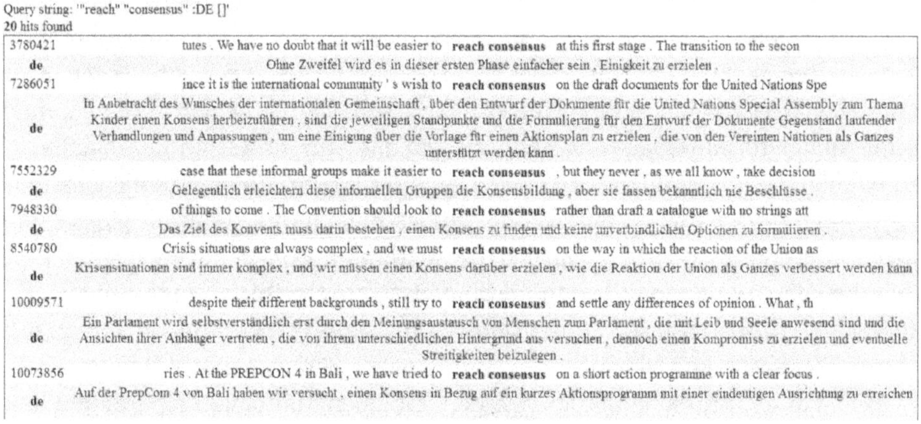

Abbildung 3: Concordancer für Parallelkorpora am Beispiel von Opus-Corpus

Im Gegensatz zu den in §6.1.1 beschriebenen einsprachigen Fachkorpora, die ad-hoc für jedes neue Thema automatisch erstellt werden, integriert CorpusMode in die Software bereits aufbereitete Parallelkorpora. Der Grund liegt darin, dass es sehr aufwendig ist, frei verfügbare Texte im Web aufzubereiten und zu alignieren. Als Korpusquelle dient das Open Source Parallel Corpus[27]. Im OPUS-Korpus wurden frei zugänglich mehrsprachige Internetressourcen aligniert und in einem standardisierten XML-Format (TMX) als Downloaddatei zur Verfügung gestellt. Das Projekt stellt unterschiedliche Korpora bereit, wie z.B. *ECB - European Central Bank corpus, EMEA - European Medicines Agency documents, EURO-PARL – European Parliament Proceedings, OpenSubs – the opensubtitles.org cor-*

---

[27] http://opus.lingfil.uu.se/

pus, etc. Die Korpora sind nicht linguistisch annotiert.[28] Die Suchmöglichkeiten bestehen daher aus reinen Zeichenketten. Zusammen mit den automatisch erstellten Korpora und den weiteren linguistischen Ressourcen (siehe §6.1.4 und §6.1.5) können diese Parallelkorpora als zusätzliche Nachschlageressource verwendet werden, um sprachliche Informationen zu einem bestimmten Fachthema zu gewinnen. Vorteil der Einbindung von Parallelkorpora in CorpusMode ist die Möglichkeit, gezielt Übersetzungsvorschläge (z.B. Terminologie, Phraseologie, etc.) in dem gerade verwendeten Sprachpaar zu erhalten. Es sei an dieser Stelle angemerkt, dass CorpusMode in erster Linie für die Vorbereitung fachspezifischer Konferenzen gedacht ist. Die zur Zeit verfügbaren Parallelkorpora sind allerdings eher allgemeinsprachlicher Natur und können daher nicht alle möglichen Domänen abdecken. Obwohl die Zahl der frei verfügbaren Parallelkorpora in absehbarer Zeit steigen wird, wird sich ihr Nutzen weiterhin auf die Analyse allgemeinsprachlicher Phänomene beschränken. Dennoch kann dies für Dolmetscher von besonderer Bedeutung sein, vor allem im Hinblick auf die Suche nach Äquivalenzen in der Fremdsprache (Fantinuoli 2006).

6.1.4 Definitionen und Übersetzungsvorschläge für Fachtermini

Ein Korpus kann eine unerschöpfliche Quelle inhaltlicher und sprachlicher Informationen über ein Themengebiet sein. Es ist allerdings nicht immer die beste Ressource, wenn man z.B. nur nach der Definition eines Wortes sucht, wie Partington beobachtet:

> Corpus examples give only contextual clues, from which it is not always easy to reconstruct the conceptual meaning of a word precisely, since speakers and writers tend to take it for granted that the hearer or reader will have a good idea of the conceptual meaning of most words used (2001: 64).

Um das Informationsangebot aus der Korpusanalyse zu ergänzen, können auf der graphischen Benutzeroberfläche Zusatzinformationen zu einem Wort dargestellt werden. Das Web bietet nicht nur eine fast unendliche Anzahl an Texten, die zum Aufbau eines Korpus benutzt werden können; es stellt auch Informationen zur Verfügung, die für die Vorbereitung eines Dolmetscheinsatzes geeignet sind und schon heute zum Alltag eines jeden Dolmetschers gehören. Darunter fallen z.B. Enzyklopädien, Wörterbücher, terminologische Datenbanken, Expertenforen, etc. Das so genannte Web 2.0 erlebt seit einigen Jahren einen regelrechten

---

[28] Für einen Überblick über linguistisch annotierte Parallelkorpora (Treebanken) siehe z.B. Hansen-Schirra & Čulo (2009).

Boom. Dabei handelt es sich um eine neue Generation des Webs, die durch eine Reihe interaktiver und kollaborativer Elemente charakterisiert ist. Durch den aktiven Beitrag der Webcommunity werden Webseiten zu *Knowledge Repositories*, aus denen zahlreiche Informationen automatisch gewonnen werden können.[29]

Zu den bekanntesten Web 2.0 Internetseiten gehört zweifelsohne Wikipedia,[30] deren Ziel der „Aufbau einer Universalenzyklopädie durch freiwillige und ehrenamtliche Autoren" ist. Die große Anzahl der Artikel (die deutsche Version zählte Ende 2010 ca. 1.135.000 Artikel[31]) stellt zusammen mit ihrer Interkonnektivität die Stärke dieses Dienstes dar. Wikipedia und ähnliche enzyklopädische Seiten bieten Dolmetschern die Möglichkeit, sich rasch in ein Thema einzuarbeiten und damit „a mental representation of incoming text on the basis of previous knowledge" (Kalina 2005: 777) zu bilden. Der Mangel an Maßnahmen zur Qualitätssicherung der Beiträge wird allerdings von mehreren Wissenschaftlern bemängelt, so dass Nutzer dieser Ressource oft kritisch gegenüber stehen. So prüfte Lorenz (2009) in der deutschsprachigen Wikipedia z.B. alle 285 Einträge zum Thema Zahnmedizin auf ihre medizinisch-wissenschaftliche Qualität. 16% der Artikel enthielten demnach inhaltliche Fehler und waren nicht geeignet, aktuelles zahnmedizinisches Fachwissen zu verbreiten. Der Rest wurde als qualitativ mit einem Lehrbuch vergleichbar eingestuft (28%) oder vermittelte richtiges Wissen, ohne jedoch von der Qualität der Darstellung her einem Lehrbuch ebenbürtig zu sein (56%). Diese Untersuchung zeigt, dass trotz der unwiderlegbaren Problematik eines Teils der Artikel 84% der Informationen brauchbar sind. Eine offene Plattform wie Wikipedia kann demnach als geeignete Informationsquelle betrachtet werden. Der Gebrauch solcher Informationen seitens der Dolmetscher dient im Grunde genommen jedoch ohnehin nur der Aneignung eines Grundwissens, die es ihnen ermöglicht, konferenzspezifische Texte zu verstehen. Die verschiedenen Perspektiven eines Anwenders, der Wikipedia als Einstieg in ein Thema verwendet, und eines anderen Nutzers, der nicht nur einen Überblick über die Begrifflichkeit bekommen möchte, sondern die konkreten Informationen in seine Arbeit einbeziehen bzw. umsetzen möchte (z.B. ein Arzt), relativiert die Gewichtung qualitativ nicht hochwertiger Artikel.

Über diese offenen, kollaborativen Angebote hinaus bieten viele Internetseiten außerdem Zugang zu traditionellen Wörterbüchern und lexikalischen Datenbanken, die im Umfang kleiner als Web 2.0 Anwendungen sind, aber einen hohen

---

[29] Für weitere Informationen zum Einsatz von Web 2.0 für NPL siehe z.B. (Frank, Reiter & Hartung 2008).

[30] http://www.wikipedia.org

[31] Dieser Wert basiert auf der Angabe von Wikipedia, abrufbar unter http://de.wikipedia.org/wiki/Wikipedia:%C3%9Cber_Wikipedia (abgerufen am 15.10.2010)

Qualitätsanspruch haben. Als Beispiel kann an dieser Stelle das englische Word-Net[32] der Universität Princeton erwähnt werden.

Wie die oben aufgeführten enzyklopädischen und lexikalischen Informations-quellen ist auch die Zahl der Online-Ressourcen, die Übersetzungen von Termini anbieten, sehr groß. Man denke z.B. an die Internetseiten BEOLINGUS der TU Chemnitz[33], leo.de[34], dict.cc[35] oder IATE[36], die mehrsprachige Terminologie-Da-tenbank der Europäischen Union. Auch hier gelten dieselben Einschränkungen zur Qualität, die man bei enzyklopädischen Ressourcen wie Wikipedia feststellen muss. Dennoch bieten sie dem professionellen Sprachmittler Übersetzungsvor-schläge, die als Basis für eine weiterführende terminologische Recherche dienen können.

All diese Ressourcen werden heutzutage von den meisten Dolmetschern schon eingesetzt. Da sie in vielen Fällen unter einer Creative-Commons-Lizenz sowie ei-ner GNU-Lizenz für freie Dokumentation freigegeben sind (wie z.B. Wikipedia), ist es möglich, diese Informationen in eine einzige Benutzeroberfläche zu bün-deln und mit vorhandenen zusätzlichen Ressourcen, etwa die extrahierte Fach-terminologie, zu kombinieren. Ausgehend von einem konferenzrelevanten Ter-minus kann der Nutzer somit direkt auf Definitionen und Übersetzungsvorschlä-ge zugreifen, die ihn bei der inhaltlichen und sprachlichen Vorbereitung unter-stützen können.

6.1.5 Verwandte Termini und Kollokationen

Durch die Visualisierung eines semantischen Netzes, das ausgehend von einem *Node* verwandte Worte abbildet, können Brainstorming-Aktivitäten gefördert werden. Brainstorming ist eine Strategie, die verwendet wird, um bereits gespei-cherte Informationen im Gehirn zu aktivieren oder um Wissen durch neue In-formationen zu erweitern. Dies geschieht, indem man assoziativ an Begriffe und Benennungen denkt, die mit einem Ausgangsthema semantisch und inhaltlich verwandt sind (Osborn 1957). Dieser Ansatz des assoziativen Lernens kann in ei-nem den Dolmetschern nicht vertrauten Thema durch die Bereitstellung thema-tisch verwandter Begriffe und Kollokationen erfolgen.[37] Zock, Ferret & Schwab

---

[32] http://wordnet.princeton.edu/

[33] http://dict.tu-chemnitz.de

[34] http://www.leo.de

[35] http://www.dict.cc

[36] http://iate.europa.eu

[37] Zur Rolle des Brainstorming bei der interlingualen Übersetzung, dem Zugang zu „common concepts" und der „activation of concepts", Blot, Zárate & Paulus (2003).

argumentiert, dass „Information access depends crucially on the organization of the data (words) and the access keys (meaning/form), two factors largely overlooked" (2010: 201). Um dieses Problem zu überwinden, bietet sich die Anwendung von Wordclouds an, die den Zugang zu neuen Termini erleichtern und dynamischer gestalten können.

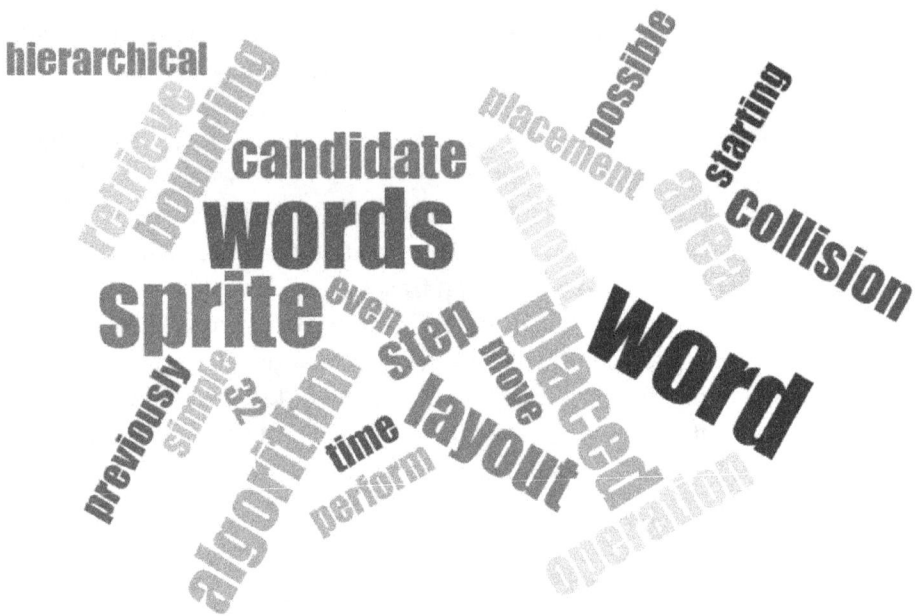

Abbildung 4: Wordcloud

Ein semantisches Netz, das als Ausgangspunkt einen extrahierten Fachterminus hat, lässt sich beispielsweise bilden, indem man die Vernetzung der Einträge in Wikipedia nutzt, um semantisch verwandte Wörter zu extrahieren. Durch das Parsing des HTML-Codes eines bestimmten Eintrages ist es möglich, alle als Link markierten Benennungen zu identifizieren und als Grundlage für die Darstellung des semantisches Netzes zu verwenden. Da diese Wörter von der Wikipedia-Community als Links zu weiterführenden Artikeln markiert wurden, sind sie de facto Termini, die mit dem Node – d.h. dem ursprünglichen Artikel – verwandt sind. Diese Brainstorming-Aktivität kann auch durch die Bereitstellung von Kollokationen ergänzt werden, denn:

Ein standardmäßiges Nachschlagen in der aufkommenden Gattung von Kollokationswörterbüchern mit einem Vorschlag der üblichsten Kollokatoren wird sicherlich die Antizipation beim Simultandolmetschen erleichtern, ebenso wie die Differenzierungsfähigkeit (Stoll 2009: 58).

Die Art der Darstellung dieser Termini ist in Abb. 4 zu sehen. Die einzelnen Termini fungieren demnach als „Access Keys" bzw. als „an index based on the notion of association" (Zock, Ferret & Schwab 2010: 201), um das Thema der Konferenz weiter zu vertiefen oder um bereits vorhandene Kenntnisse vor einem Einsatz wieder zu aktivieren.

6.2 Terminologie verwalten: TermMode

Während terminologische Daten und fachliche Informationen lange Zeit auf Papier verfasst und verbreitet wurden, bieten computerlinguistische Anwendungen und das Internet neue Möglichkeiten der Datenverarbeitung und -darstellung. Die Verfügbarkeit großer Datenmengen, die dynamische Datendarstellung und die unterschiedlichsten Möglichkeiten des Datenzugriffs mittels ausgereifter Suchverfahren sind nur einige der wichtigen Vorteile der elektronischen Datenverarbeitung.

Die starre und meist normative Struktur gedruckter lexikografischer Werke wie z.B. Wörterbücher und Lexika überlassen den dynamischen und linguistisch deskriptiven Ansätzen der computerunterstützten Wissens- und Terminologieverwaltung das Feld. Die Vernetzung kontrollierter Datenbestände (Glossaren) mit automatisch gesammelten Fachtexten (6.1.1) sowie die Einbindung von Datensammlungen in speziell für die Bedürfnisse der Nutzer programmierten Anwendungen (§6.1.4 und §6.1.5) können die Möglichkeiten der *Knowledge Experience* – der Aneignung von Wissen und Terminologie – erweitern und ergänzen (Fantinuoli 2009).

In diesem Zusammenhang kommt das Terminologieverwaltungsmodul von InterpretBank namens TermMode zum Einsatz. Mehrsprachige Glossare werden in einer SQLite-Datenbank gespeichert. Neben der Möglichkeit, eine Benennung in mehreren Sprachen zu registrieren, ermöglicht die Software es auch, weitere Informationen zu einem Begriff zu speichern wie z.B. Kollokationen, Definitionen, etc. Alle Glossare werden in einer einzigen Datenbank verwaltet und mittels zweier Klassifikatoren gegliedert, nämlich *Glossar* und *Konferenz*. Speziell auf die Dolmetscher zugeschnittene Felder sind in der Benutzeroberfläche integriert; so kann das Feld *ConfInfo* z.B. dazu genutzt werden, simultanrelevante Informationen zu speichern, um diese in der Kabine mit ConferenceMode zusammen mit den Benennungen abzurufen.

Die ergonomische Darstellungsstruktur ist modularisiert, d.h. an die jeweiligen Bedürfnisse des Nutzers anpassbar. Somit kann die Bedienungsoberfläche geändert werden: Von einer vereinfachten Eintragsstruktur, in der nur die jeweiligen Benennungen eingetragen werden können (Abb. 5), in eine komplexere Struktur, die es erlaubt, Zusatzinformationen zu einem Begriff einzugeben (Abb. 6). Diese Expansionsfähigkeit ist stufenweise einstellbar.

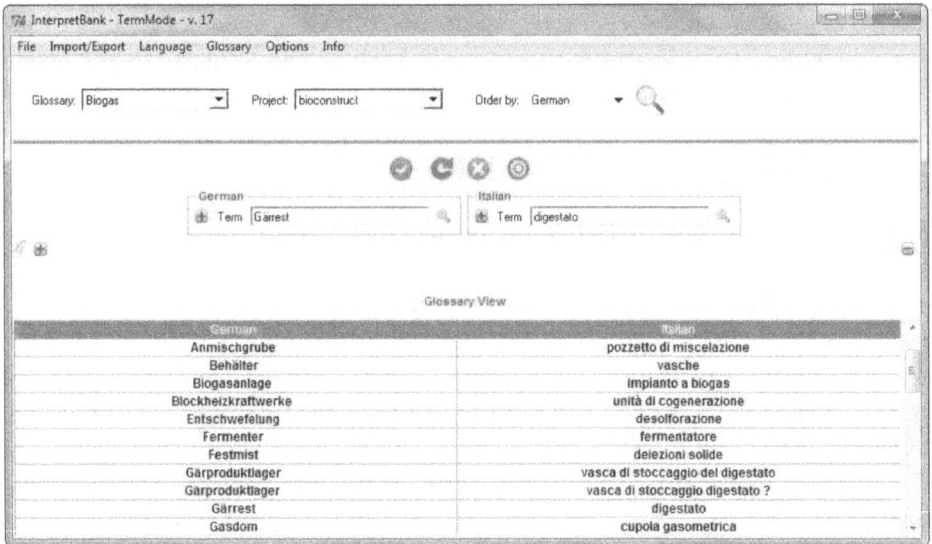

Abbildung 5: TermMode, einfache Eintragungsstruktur

Die Visualisierung der Glossare erfolgt in tabellarischer Form und entspricht somit der klassischen Darstellungsform, wie sie von Dolmetschern und Übersetzern typischerweise für ihre Glossare verwendet wird. Darüber hinaus ist das Modul mit CorpusMode dynamisch verbunden: Die Termkandidaten, die von einem Fachkorpus extrahiert wurden, können z.B. automatisch in TermMode importiert werden. Außerdem kann der Nutzer, ausgehend von einem Eintrag im Glossar, zusätzliche Informationen wie Konkordanzen, Definitionen, verwandte Wörter, usw. direkt in TermMode abrufen. Anders als bei traditionellen Terminologieverwaltungssystemen wird so der Zugang zur Terminologie mit TermMode dynamischer: Die Informationen, die dem Nutzer zur Verfügung stehen, sind nicht mehr nur auf diejenigen Informationen beschränkt, die man in eine klassische Eintragungsstruktur manuell eingepflegt hat, sondern werden durch die projektbezogenen Ressourcen erweitert, die durch CorpusMode bereit gestellt wurden.

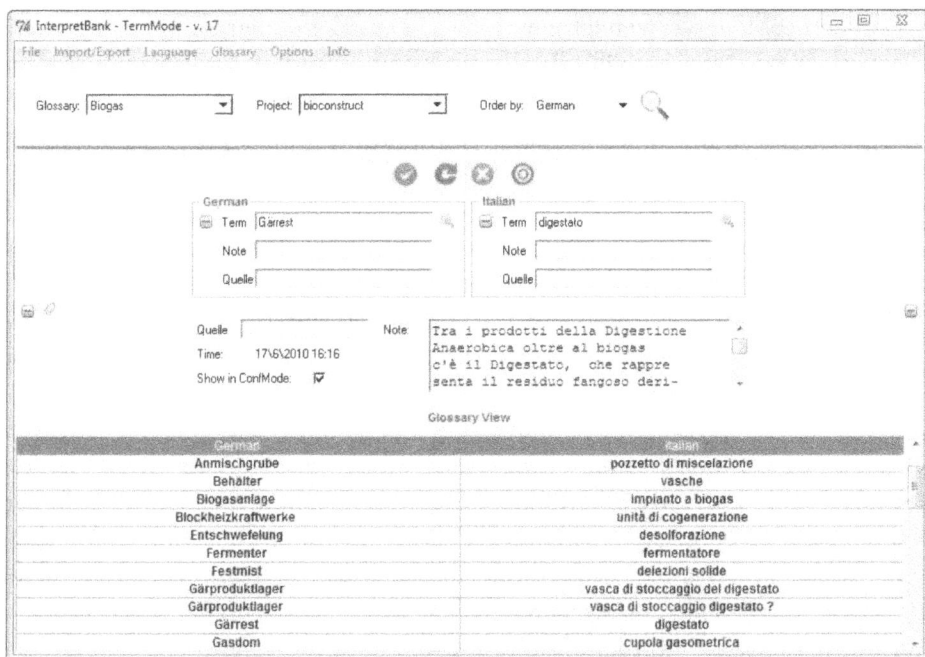

Abbildung 6: TermMode, erweiterte Eintragungsstruktur

6.3 Terminologie abrufen: ConferenceMode

ConferenceMode ermöglicht Konferenzdolmetschern in der Kabine den schnellen und bedarfsorientierten Zugriff auf bestehende mehrsprachige Terminologiedaten, d.h. auch während der Verdolmetschung. Aufgrund der Besonderheiten des Dolmetschprozesses in einer Simultansituation muss die Anwendung für den Einsatz in der Kabine vor allem Wert auf die folgenden Grundbeschaffenheiten legen (Sprachen and Dolmetscher Institut München 2007):

- schnelle und flexible Suchfunktion

- Übersichtlichkeit

- komfortable und schnelle Eingabe neuer Termini

- intuitive Bedienbarkeit

- Kompatibilität mit anderen Programmen

ConferenceMode verwendet eine interne Datenbank, das so genannte *Activ Glossary*. Diese Datei enthält alle Wortpaare und Zusatzinformationen, die im Vorfeld für einen Einsatz geladen wurden und bleibt unverändert, bis ConferenceMode für den nächsten Einsatz mit einem anderen Glossar geladen wird. Diese Lösung ermöglicht es Dolmetschern, das *activ Glossary* individuell zusammenzustellen, indem sie ein oder mehrere Glossare aus TermMode oder aus anderen Programmen (MS Word, MS Excel, SDL Multiterm, etc.) nacheinander laden. Dank dieser hohen Flexibilität können Dolmetscher sogar am Einsatzort schnell und unproblematisch Glossare von Kunden oder Kollegen einlesen und zum aktiven Glossar hinzufügen, ohne komplizierte Importfunktionen durchführen zu müssen.

Die Idee, Fachglossare auch während der Verdolmetschung nachzuschlagen, ist nicht neu (Stoll 2002) und wird einerseits durch die Vorverlagerung der kognitiven Prozesse in die Vorbereitungsphase ermöglicht – was die Dolmetscher während der Verdolmetschung entlastet (siehe §2) – andererseits durch die Tatsache, dass Dolmetscher die Einträge eines Glossars (meist) selbst in das Terminologieverwaltungssystem eingetragen haben, wobei „die gefundenen Äquivalenzen nur noch reaktiviert" werden (Drechsel 2005: 18). ConferenceMode fungiert somit eher als eine Gedächtnisstütze denn als Gedächtnisersatz.

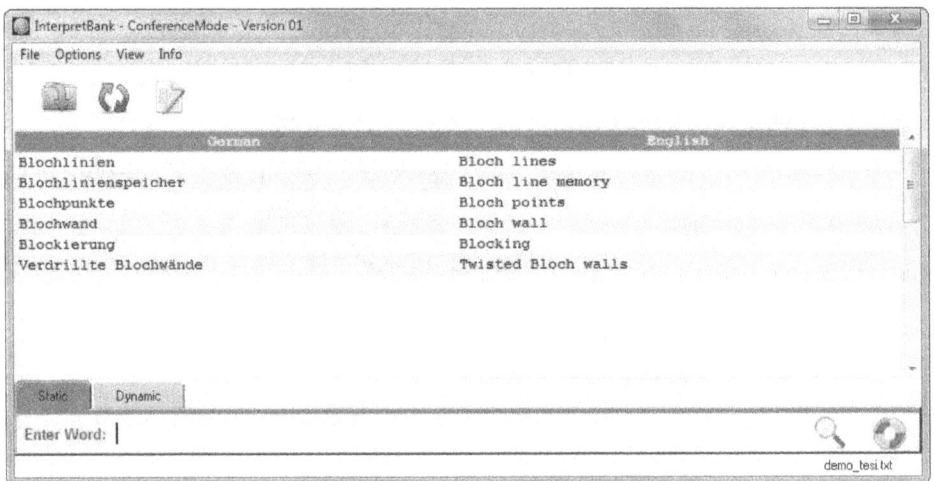

Abbildung 7: ConferenceMode, kabinenfreundliches Nachschlagen während der Konferenz

Um den Dolmetschprozess so wenig wie möglich zu beeinträchtigen und die Dolmetscher bei der Suche nach passenden Fachbegriffen auch während der Verdolmetschung optimal zu unterstützen, ist es notwendig, den kognitiven Aufwand für die Benutzung des Tools niedrig zu halten. Dafür muss einerseits der erforderliche Input seitens des Nutzers so klein wie möglich sein, andererseits muss der Output, d.h. die Ergebnisse einer Suchoperation, so übersichtlich wie möglich dargestellt und in der Anzahl auf ein Minimum reduziert werden. Idealerweise sollten die Dolmetscher also mit wenig Aufwand möglichst wenige, aber gleichzeitig relevante Treffer angezeigt bekommen, damit sie von der Suchoperation nicht abgelenkt werden. In ConferenceMode wird der gesuchte Begriff mittels Tastatur eingegeben, während die Suche mit der Entertaste oder mit einem Suchalgorithmus (ohne Entertaste) begonnen wird. Der Suchalgorithmus ermöglicht das Anzeigen der relevanten Treffer schon während der Eingabe. Bei jedem neuen Buchstaben, der eingetippt wird, werden die Ergebnisse entsprechend reduziert. Sobald die voreingestellte Anzahl von Treffern angezeigt wird (standardmäßig fünf Treffer), wird die Suche beendet und die Eingabemaske für eine weitere Suche freigegeben.

Die Reduzierung der angezeigten Treffer erfolgt u.a. durch den Einsatz von Stopwords. Wenn man z.B. nach dem Wort „Dermatologie" sucht und die Buchstabenkette „d", „de" oder „der" eingibt, wird der Eintrag „Entzündung der Bauchspeicheldrüse" nicht angezeigt, weil der Artikel „der" auf die Stopwordliste gesetzt wurde. Man geht dabei davon aus, dass Nutzer nur nach bedeutungstragenden Wörtern suchen, so dass sie bei dem Terminus „Entzündung der Bauchspeicheldrüse" entweder nach dem Wort „Entzündung" oder „Bauchspeicheldrüse" suchen würden. Darüber hinaus korrigiert der Suchalgorithmus mögliche Tippfehler bei der Eingabe der Zeichenkette (Suchwort) und in den Termini, die im Glossar gespeichert sind. Dafür wurde die Fuzzy-Match-Korrektur nach dem Prinzip der Levenshtein-Distanz implementiert. Aufgrund der Spontaneität der Suche und der Besonderheit der Situation, in der diese stattfindet, ermöglicht die Behebung dieser möglichen Fehlerquelle eine weitere Entlastung für die Dolmetscher, die, anders als Übersetzer, eine fehlgeschlagene Suche aus Zeitgründen nicht mehr wiederholen können. Dank dieser interaktiven Suchmethode werden Dolmetscher bei der Suche erheblich entlastet, da sie einen kleineren kognitiven Aufwand investieren müssen (Reduzierung der zu betätigenden Tasten, Darstellung nur weniger Treffer, etc.).

Während des Einsatzes haben Dolmetscher oft die Möglichkeit, ihr terminologisches Wissen durch neu gewonnene Informationen zu ergänzen. Damit die Eingabe neuer Termini während des Einsatzes schnell und komfortabel erfolgen kann, ist es möglich, auf eine dedizierte Eintragungsmaske zurückzugreifen, um neue Termini oder Anmerkungen zu schon vorhandenen Termini zu ergänzen.

Die neuen Termini werden direkt zu dem aktiven Glossar hinzugefügt, so dass diese in der Kabine gleich abrufbar sind. Zudem werden sie automatisch in Term-Mode aufgenommen, damit sie ordnungsgemäß gespeichert werden und nicht verlorenen gehen.

Abbildung 8: TermMode, schnelles Eintragen neuer Termini während der Konferenz

Wie in §6.2 erwähnt, kann die reine zweispaltige Darstellung in Conference-Mode mit den zweisprachigen Benennungen um eine dritte Spalte mit allgemeinen Informationen erweitert werden, die von den Dolmetschern als konferenzrelevant erachtet werden. In dieser Spalte können beispielsweise Informationen zur Verwendung eines Begriffs hinzugefügt werden.

Zu den weiteren Funktionen von ConferenceMode gehören die Anpassung der Suchfunktion beim bidirektionalen Dolmetschen, die Suche – durch die *EmergencySearch* – in der gesamten TermMode-Datenbank sowie die Möglichkeit, besondere Zeichen wie z.B. diakritische Zeichen bei der Suche zu ignorieren.

7 Schlusswort

Während Softwareanwendungen seit Jahren ein fester Bestandteil des Übersetzerberufs sind, bleibt die Praxis des Dolmetschens von den neuesten Entwicklungen und Erkenntnissen im Bereich Computer- und Korpuslinguistik weiterhin unberührt. Da die möglichen Vorteile des computergestützten Dolmetschens vor, während und nach der Verdolmetschung auf der Hand liegen, versucht das Projekt InterpretBank, eine erste Brücke zwischen den terminologie- und korpusorientierten Ansätzen in der Dolmetschwissenschaft und dem „state-of-the-art" in der Computerlinguistik zu schlagen, damit praktizierenden und angehenden Dolmetschern die Möglichkeit eingeräumt wird, auf ein Tool zurückgreifen zu können, das die Qualität ihrer Dienstleistung steigert.

References

Andres, Dörte. 2011. Dolmetschwissenschaft zu Beginn des 21. Jahrhunderts: Ein integrativ konzipiertes Dolmetschprozeßmodell. *LVI* (1). 81–103.

Arntz, Reiner, Heribert Picht & Felix Mayer. 2009. *Einführung in die Terminologiearbeit*. Hildesheim: Olms.

Aston, Guy. 2001. Learning with corpora: An overview. In Guy Aston (ed.), *Learning with corpora*, 4–45. Bologna: Cooperativa Libraria Universitaria Editrice.

Balboni, Paolo. 2002. *Le sfide di Babele: Insegnare le lingue nelle societe complesse*. Torino: UTET.

Baroni, Marco & Silvia Bernardini. 2004. BootCaT: Bootstrapping corpora and terms from the web. In *Proceedings of LREC2004*, 1313–1316. Lisbon: ELDA.

Bendazzoli, Claudio & Annalisa Sandrelli. 2005. An approach to corpus-based interpreting studies: Developing EPIC (European Parliament Interpreting Corpus). In Sandra Nauert (ed.), *MuTra 2005 – Challenges of Multidimensional Translation: Conference Proceedings*, 1–12. Saarbrücken.

Bernardini, Silvia. 2001. Spoilt for choice: A learner explores general language. In Guy Aston (ed.), *Learning with corpora*, 220–249. Bologna: CLUEB.

Bilgen, Baris. 2009. *Investigating terminology management for conference interpreters*. Ottawa: Faculty of Graduate & Postdoctoral Studies of the University of Ottawa PhD thesis.

Blot, Kevin J., Michal A. Zárate & Paul B. Paulus. 2003. Code-switching across brainstorming sessions: Implications for the revised hierarchical model of bilingual language processing. *Experimental Psychology (formerly Zeitschrift für Experimentelle Psychologie)* 50(3). 171–183.

Boulton, Alex. 2009. Data-Driven Learning: Reasonable fears and rational reassurance. *Indian Journal of Applied Linguistics* 35(1). 81–106.

Castagnoli, Sara. 2006. Wacky! Working papers on the Web as Corpus. In Marco Baroni & Silvia Bernardini (eds.), 159–172. Bologna: GEDIT.

Čulo, Oliver. 2011. *Automatische Extraktion von bilingualen Valenzwörterbüchern aus deutsch-englischen Parallelkorpora: Eine Pilotstudie*. Saarbrücken: universaar.

Drechsel, Alexander. 2005. Zukunftsvisionen des Computereinsatzes beim Dolmetschen. *MDÜ: Mitteilungen für Dolmetscher und Übersetzer* 6. 16–21.

Dwork, Cynthia, Ravi Kumar, Moni Naor & D. Sivakumar. 2001. Rank aggregation methods for the web. In *Proceedings of the 10th International Conference on World Wide Web*, 613–622.

Fantinuoli, Claudio. 2006. Specialized corpora from the web and term extraction for simultaneous interpreters. In Marco Baroni & Silvia Bernardini (eds.), *Wacky! Working papers on web as corpus*, 173–190. Bologna: GEDIT.

Fantinuoli, Claudio. 2009. InterpretBank: Ein Tool zum Wissens- und Terminologiemanagement für Simultandolmetscher. In Wolfram Baur, Sylvia Kalina, Felix Mayer & Jutta Witzel (eds.), *Übersetzen in die Zukunft: Herausforderungen der Globalisierung für Dolmetscher und Übersetzer*, 411–417. Berlin: BDÜ.

Feldweg, Erich. 1996. *Der Konferenzdolmetscher im internationalen Kommunikationsprozeß*. Heidelberg: Julius Groos.

Frank, Anette, Nils Reiter & Matthias Hartung. 2008. A resource-poor approach for linking ontology classes to Wikipedia articles. In *Semantics in text processing: STEP 2008 conference proceedings*, 382–387. London: College Publications.

Friedbichler, Ingrid & Michael Friedbichler. 2000. The potential of domain-specific target language corpora for the translator's workbench. In *I corpora nella didattica della traduzio ne: atti del Seminario di studi interna zionale, Bertinoro, 14-15 novembre 1997*. Bologna: CLUEB.

Friedl, Jeffrey E. F. 2006. *Mastering regular expressions*. Sebastopol: O'Reilly.

Gerzymisch-Arbogast, Heidrun. 1996. *Termini im Kontext: Verfahren zur Erschließung und übersetzung der textspezifischen Bedeutung von fachlichen Ausdrücken*. Tübingen: Narr.

Ghani, Rayid, Rosie Jones & Dunja Mladenic. 2001. Mining the web to create minority language corpora. In *Conference on information and knowledge management*, 279–286. Atlanta, Georgia, USA: ACM.

Gile, Daniel. 1995. *Basic concepts and models for translators and interpreter training*. Amsterdam & Philadelphia: John Benjamins.

Gorjanc, Vojko. 2009. Terminology resources and terminological data management for medical interpreters. In Dörte Andres & Sonja Pöllabauer (eds.), *Spürst Du, wie der Bauch rauf-runter? Fachdolmetschen im Gesundheitsbereich. Is everything all topsy turvy in your tummy? Healthcare Interpreting*, 85–95. München: Meidenbauer.

Gross-Dinter, Ursula. 2009. Konferenzdolmetschen und Community Interpreting: Schritte zu einer Partnerschaft. In Wolfram Baur, Sylvia Kalina, Felix Mayer & Jutta Witzel (eds.), *Übersetzen in die Zukunft: Herausforderungen der Globalisierung für Dolmetscher und Übersetzer*, 354–362. Berlin: BDÜ.

Hansen-Schirra, Silvia & Elke Teich. 2008. Corpora in human translation. In Merja Kytö & Anke Lüdeling (eds.), *Corpus linguistics: An international handbook*, 1159–1175. Berlin, New York: de Gruyter.

Hansen-Schirra, Silvia & Oliver Čulo. 2009. Lost in translation annotation: Limitations of flat parallel corpora – expectations of parallel treebanks. In *Gscl workshop: Linguistic processing pipelines*. Potsdam.

Honegger, Monica. 2006. *Die Anwendung von Terminologiesystemen beim Simultandolmetschen*. Winterthur: Institut für Übersetzen und Dolmetschen Zürcher Hochschule Winterthur.

Johns, Tim. 1988. Whence and whither classroom concordancing? In Theo Bongaerts (ed.), *Computer applications in language learning*, 9–32. Dordrecht: Foris.

Johns, Tim. 1991. Should you be persuaded: Two examples of data-driven learning. *English Language Research Journal* 4. University of Birmingham, 1–16.

Johns, Tim. 1994. From printout to handout: Grammar and vocabulary teaching in the context of Data-driven Learning. In Terence Odlin (ed.), *Perspectives on Pedagogical Grammar*, 293–313. Cambridge: Cambridge University Press.

Kalina, Sylvia. 2001. Zur Professionalisierung beim Dolmetschen. Vorschläge für Forschung und Lehre. In Andreas Kelletat (ed.), *Dolmetschen: Beiträge aus Forschung, Lehre und Praxis*, 51–64. Frankfurt am Main: Peter Lang.

Kalina, Sylvia. 2005. Quality assurance for interpreting processes. *Meta* 50(2). 769–784.

Kalina, Sylvia. 2007. Microphone off – application of the process model of interpreting to the classroom. *Kalbotyra* 57(3). 111–121.

Kilgarriff, Adam & Gregory Grefenstette. 2003. Introduction to the special issue on the web as corpus. *Computational Linguistics* 29(3). 333–347.

Kiraly, Donald C. 2000. *Social constructivist approach to translator education: Empowerment from theory to practice*. Manchester: St. Jerome.

Lemnitzer, Lothar & Heike Zinsmeister. 2010. *Korpuslinguistik: Eine Einführung*. Tübingen: Narr.

Lorenz, Annette. 2009. *Beurteilung der Qualität zahnmedizinischer Einträge in Wikipedia – ein Vergleich mit zahnmedizinischer Fachliteratur*. Freiburg (Breisgau): Albert-Ludwigs-Universität Freiburg PhD thesis. http://www.freidok.uni-freiburg.de/volltexte/6884/.

Meyer, Bernd. 2008. Interpreting proper names: Different interventions in simultaneous and consecutive interpreting? *trans-kom* 1(1). 105–122.

Meyer, Bernd, Kristin Bührig, Ortrun Kliche & Birte Pawlack. 2010. Nurses as interpreters: Aspects of interpreter training for bilingual medical employees. In Bernd Meyer & Birgit Apfelbaum (eds.), *Multilingualism at work: From policies to practices in public, medical, and business settings*, 163–184. Amsterdam: John Benjamins.

Osborn, Alex Faickney. 1957. *Applied imagination: Principles and procedures of creative thinking.* New York: Scribner's Sons.

Partington, Alan. 2001. Corpus-based description in teaching and learning. In Guy Aston (ed.), *Learning with corpora,* 63–84. Bologna: Cooperativa Libraria Universitaria Editrice.

Pearson, Jennifer. 2003. Using parallel texts in the translator training environment. In Federico Zanettin, Silvia Bernardini & Dominic Stewart (eds.), *Corpora in translator education,* 15–24. Manchester: St. Jerome.

Picht, Heribert. 1990. Übersetzungswissenschaft: Ergebnisse und Perspektiven. Festschrift für Wolfram Wilss zum 65. Geburtstag. In Reiner Arntz (ed.), *Die Fachwendung – Ein Stiefkind der Fachübersetzung,* 207–215. Tübingen: Narr.

Pöchhacker, Franz. 2000. *Dolmetschen – Konzeptuelle Grundlagen und deskriptive Untersuchungen.* Tübingen: Stauffenburg.

Pöchhacker, Franz. 2004. *Introducing interpreting studies.* London: Routledge.

Rayson, Paul & Roger Gariside. 2000. Comparing corpora using frequency profiling. In *Proceedings of the Workshop on Comparing Corpora,* 1–6. Hong Kong: Association for Computational Linguistics.

Rossenbeck, Klaus. 1989. Lexikologische und lexikographische Probleme fachsprachlicher Phraseologie aus konstrastiver Sicht. In Mary Snell-Hornby & Esther Pöhl (eds.), *Translation and lexicography,* 197–210. Amsterdam: John Benjamins.

Rütten, Anja. 2007. *Informations- und Wissensmanagement im Konferenzdolmetschen.* Frankfurt: Lang.

Sprachen and Dolmetscher Institut München. 2007. Terminologietools für den Einsatz in der Simultankabine. *MDÜ* 2007(3). 26ff.

Stoll, Christoph. 2002. Terminologiesysteme für Simultandolmetscher. *MDÜ: Mitteilungen für Dolmetscher und Übersetzer* 2002. 47–51.

Stoll, Christoph. 2009. *Jenseits simultanfähiger Terminologiesysteme.* Trier: Wvt Wissenschaftlicher Verlag.

Teubert, Wolfgang. 2003. Collocations, parallel corpora and language teaching. In *Selected papers from the Twelfth International Symposium on English.* Taipei.

Ueyama, Motoko. 2006. Evaluation of japanese web-based reference corpora: Effects of seed selection and time interval. In Marco Baroni & Silvia Bernardini (eds.), *Wacky! Working papers on web as corpus,* 99–126. Bologna: GEDIT.

Valentini, Cristina. 2002. *Uso del computer in cabina di interpretazione.* Bologna: SSLiMIT Forlì , Università di Bologna PhD thesis.

Varantola, Krista. 2003. Corpora in translator education. In Federica Zanettin, Silvia Bernardini & Dominic Stewart (eds.), *Translators and disposable corpora*, 55–70. Manchester: St Jerome.

Will, Martin. 2009. *Dolmetschorientierte Terminologiearbeit: Modell und Methode*. Tübingen: Gunter Narr.

Will, Martin. 2010. Vom Wort zum Wissen und zurück. *MDÜ: Mitteilungen für Dolmetscher und Übersetzer* 3. 52–57.

Zanettin, Federico. 2002. In Elia Yuste-Rodrigo (ed.), *Language resources for translation work and research*, 10–14. Corpora in translation practice. Las Palmas de Gran Canaria: LREC 2002 Workshop Proceedings.

Zock, Michael, Olivier Ferret & Didier Schwab. 2010. Deliberate word access: An intuition, a roadmap and some preliminary empirical results. *International Journal of Speech Technology* 13(4). 201–218.

Name index

Name index

Subject index

www.ingramcontent.com/pod-product-compliance
Lightning Source LLC
Chambersburg PA
CBHW081225190326
41458CB00016B/5680